THE BRINK
OF FREEDOM

HOW MASOUD BARZANI TOOK KURDISTAN
TO THE EDGE OF INDEPENDENCE

DAVAN YAHYA KHALIL

The Brink of Freedom
How Masoud Barzani Took Kurdistan to the Edge of Independence

ISBN 978-1-5136-6755-3

Manufactured in the UK

Cover Design: Jason Orr
Interior Design: Kimberly Martin
Author Photograph: Irena Górniak
Interior and cover design by Jera Publishing

CONTENTS

CONTENTS

Introduction

It's too late to change the mistakes of the past, but now is a time to think of the future, and make decisions ourselves. — *Masoud Barzani*

WHEN IT COMES to Kurdistan, the case for writing about Masoud Barzani almost doesn't need to be made. Not only was he Kurdistan's president for many years, but he is also the son of one of its most famous figures, was crucially involved in its fight for independence, and was a part of almost all of the key events that have shaped it as a region in the last few decades. In recent times, he has been a key ally in the world's fight against ISIS, and has also been crucial in putting Kurdistan on the world stage.

Even more importantly, he is also the man who brought Kurdistan closer to being independent than any other. While the referendum of 2017 is now seen as a failure, Masoud Barzani succeeded in gaining almost total support for the prospect of independence among the people of the region. For one brief

1

moment, it seemed as if he might actually lead Kurdistan into a position as a self-governing state.

There is another reason to study Masoud Barzani's life: because doing so helps us to understand something about Kurdistan as a whole, about the struggles it has faced and about the ways it sees itself within the world. Almost from the moment he was born, Masoud Barzani has been a part of the story that Kurdistan tells about itself, its ambitions, and its people. His career as a peshmerga, and then as a politician, has reflected the situation within Kurdistan, and allows us to touch on the crucial issues affecting the region.

It would be impossible to write a history of Kurdistan without Masoud Barzani. Equally, understanding his life may allow us to understand the situation that Kurdistan presently finds itself in. To understand both, we will explore Masoud Barzani's childhood, his role at his father's side, his rise to leadership within the KDP, the deadly struggles of the 1980s, the role he played in the Kurdistan of the 1990s, and eventually his rise to president. We will explore his actions as Kurdistan's most important political figure, and put the referendum into its proper context.

We will do all of that, but to succeed in any of it, we need to understand more about Kurdistan's past, and the circumstances that would shape the direction of Masoud Barzani's life, even before he was born...

CHAPTER ONE

History

GREAT HISTORICAL FIGURES do not come from nowhere; they exist in a world whose conditions allow, or require, them to act. They exist, not as individual threads, but as part of a vast tapestry of human endeavour, where every action requires context, and every decision is affected by the decisions of thousands of people before them. There is even a school of thought that suggests that all our actions may be no more than the inevitable consequences of our past. This may be going too far, in denying all concept of individual agency, but it is true that no individual can truly be understood without making the effort to comprehend their historical context.

This is as true for Masoud Barzani as for any other leader, but it is precisely with such leaders that we are inclined to forget this truth. Shakespeare wrote Caesar as having a servant walk beside him, reminding him that he was but a man, but it is often not just leaders who need reminding of such things. We tend to think about leaders in a way that excludes all of the people around them, all of the ones who went before, and all of the situations that drove them to act as they did. A leader achieving something alone makes for a better story than the great wash of historical context, but we *need* that context. As much as anything, we require it to really understand to what extent an individual made a difference, to show what was uniquely them, and what would have been done by someone even if they had not been there.

For Kurdistan, that context starts a centuries ago, because of the extensive inhabited history of the region. Kurdistan, in a much larger, broader sense than the modern region, represents one of the oldest permanently settled regions in the world. There is general agreement that it was one of the earliest places to adopt agriculture as a way of life, as opposed to the hunter gathering that had gone before. It is a space that was once divided between a number of the ancient Mesopotamian civilisations, including the Babylonians, Assyrians, and Sumerians. Those civilizations were some of the most advanced in the world at the time, and their advances in writing, mathematics, measuring time and other areas have had knock on effects that continue to affect the world today.

As early as 4000 BCE, Kurdistan's current capital, Erbil, was in existence, then under the name of Hawler. While we cannot prove a direct connection between the societies of then and today, it *has* been in continuous occupation since, under a wide variety of rulers, and in various different forms, making it one of the oldest continuously inhabited cities on the planet.

In this sense, nothing can happen in Kurdistan without some sense of history standing behind it. Everything done in the region is done with the knowledge that people were there long before any person or political structure of today, speaking in the echoes of their voices, and walking in their footsteps.

We cannot say with any certainty that the people of the region at that time were Kurds as we know them today; references to those as a separate, defined ethnic group came later. There are theories, albeit unprovable ones, that the Kurds may be linked to the Medes of antiquity, who were early inhabitants of Persia. There are more tangible references to possible Kurds that are surprisingly early, with Xenophon's account of Alexander the Great mentioning "Carduchoi" who fought for the Persian Emperor, Xerxes, as early as 401 BCE. Even in these early days, there was an attempt to portray Kurds as a warlike people, whose main role in history would be to fight other people's battles. By the time of this battle, what is now Kurdistan would have been under Persian control for approximately 200 years, taken from the Babylonians.

This Persian control is important, partly because it started the tradition of Kurdish soldiers being used for the aims of bigger empires, without the prospect of their own lands, and partly because it established several of the general administrative areas into which Kurdistan finds itself divided even now.

Probably the most significant historical change in the region was the introduction of Islam from 637 onwards. It also coincided with the first use of the word "Kurds" to describe the inhabitants of the region, with Arab scholars using the term to denote the people in the mountains, resisting Islam's advance until they finally began to convert. This story of resisting a largely Arab surrounding region with the advantage of terrain but the disadvantages of numbers was one that would play out again and again in the ensuing centuries, even into the modern period.

Because the Kurds had largely converted to Islam, this opened up opportunities for some to find positions of authority in an otherwise Arab dominated region. Dynasties such as the Shaddadids, the Rawwidids, the Marwanids and the Hasanwayhids all ruled over self-ruling kingdoms in the 11th and 12th centuries, starting to fall apart with the efforts of the Turkish Seljuk dynasty to expand and gain hegemony over the region.

Again, Kurdish figures found themselves able to thrive and achieve importance within an environment that wasn't theirs. Perhaps the most famous example of this is Saladin, the founder of the Ayyubid dynasty and notable war leader who defeated the Third Crusade. His dynasty's empire might in some ways be seen as the height of Kurdish power. At the same time, we might note that in ensuing histories, his Kurdish identity has largely been erased outside of Kurdistan.

In any case, the empire that Saladin founded did not last long, overthrown by Turkish Mamluk soldiers, initially in Egypt, but then more widely as Mongol invasions weakened them. The conflict between the Mongols and the Mamluk Turks proved the salvation of the small remaining Kurdish areas, though, because it meant that they saw the need for Kurdish mercenaries and fighters to aid against their enemies. Once more, the Kurds found themselves pressed into wars that essentially were not their own, fighting under a variety of dynasties, even when the Turkmen houses replaced the conflict between the Mongols and the Turks.

This ongoing conflict proved to be the normal state of affairs until around 1500, with a series of smaller Kurdish states ruled by separate princes, all broadly under the control of the Persian Empire.

The empires shifted around the Kurds, but their position within them stayed broadly similar. Even when the Ottoman Empire expanded to take over from where the others had left off, Kurdish princes and their lands still had a role to play in providing soldiers, fighting against mutual enemies. While there was a role for them, though, there was no sense of autonomy, and they found their lands completely subsumed into the Ottoman Empire by the mid nineteenth century.

When World War One rippled out over the world, the Ottomans picked the side of Germany and the Austro-Hungarian Empire, bound up with them by the many treaties that dragged so much of the world into what could have been a smaller confrontation. The inhabitants of the Kurdistan region should, in theory, have sided with their Ottoman rulers, but instead, they took the opportunity to rise up in rebellion.

They did so partly at the behest of the British Empire and its allies, who had reasoned that the best way to limit Ottoman efforts was to light the fires of revolt behind them. It worked well, reducing the impact of the Ottomans on other fronts and contributing to the overall war effort. It, and actions like it, also served to destabilize many of the great empires that were building up around the world.

We can see this as being at least some of the point of the war. While the spark for it may have been the assassination of Archduke Franz Ferdinand, the bigger picture was one of large, existing empires and newer, growing ones pushing up against one another, all ignoring the effects on the people who actually lived in the territories they claimed. Many of them initially welcomed the war as a kind of reshuffling of the international deck, each assuming that it would be over quickly, with them holding all the cards. Each was unprepared for the kind of modern, mechanised warfare that followed, having previously been the ones employing those methods against their colonies, rather than the ones on the receiving end.

In this slower, more attrition-based war, eroding the opposition's will and supplies became part of the core strategy nations employed. Rebellions out in the hinterlands of each empire represented a good way of drawing men and resources away from other fronts, and also became a way of freeing up tracts of land from an empire's control so that they could be snatched by the next incomer.

The British Empire did much of this within the current Middle East towards the end of World War One. There was a kind of logic to it, but it was the kind of logic that only really made sense to the Great Powers of the time: if they didn't snatch it, someone else would, and then they would be at a strategic disadvantage.

This was the same logic that had prevailed through much of the nineteenth century, and perhaps before, where the outright, racist rapaciousness of "We're stronger than you, and we're white, so why shouldn't we take control of your country and its resources, for your own good?" had given way to "This territory exists on the fringes of what we already own, or near our trade routes/supply lines, so if we don't control it, others will use it to attack us". Similar logic was used as an excuse for the British invasion of Burma in 1885, where attacks across the borders into India paved the way for expansionism as a supposedly defensive move. It was an age that demanded pretext, rather than an outright land grab, but pretexts could always be found.

In the First World War, the pretext was simply that the Ottomans or Germany would control whatever Britain didn't, using the resources there to maintain their war efforts. The British moved in, and showed no signs of leaving. At the conclusion of the war, they even began the creation of an essentially artificial country, with no existing history and no reason for being beyond a desire to balance out the influence of Iran in the region: they created Iraq and installed King Faisal as its ruler.

The result of the British influence was rebellion. Sheik Mahmoud Barzanji began a rebellion against British rule as early as 1919 that focused on attacking symbols of encroaching authority such as police stations. He suspended the rebellion in 1920 though, when the Treaty of Sevres was concluded in the wake of the war.

The Treaty of Sevres represents one of the great moments of promise for Kurdistan, but is also best known as a *broken* promise. To some extent, it fuelled many of the conflicts to follow in the region. The 1920 text was largely concerned with extending the work of the 1919 Treaty of Versailles to address the aftermath of the war, arranging the disposition of territories hat had formerly belonged to the now collapsed empires of the war's losers.

Part of the treaty was the stipulation that the Kurdish people should have their own state, although it was couched in somewhat patronising language by suggesting that it should happen only when the League of Nations felt that they had advanced to the point of being ready for it, and the state that ensued would probably have continued to be under British patronage, or more correctly control, in the way that Iraq was.

It was a long way from what modern Kurdistan views as independence, but it was still a state that would be recognised by the international community and would have provided a home for Kurds. For a brief period, it seemed possible, and that was enough to convince Sheik Mahmoud Barzanji to limit his attacks, while also pulling some of his allies from him. One result of this was that he was able to be arrested in 1921, and exiled to India.

The Treaty of Sevres was never ratified, instead being replaced by the 1923 Treaty of Lausanne, which made no mention of a Kurdish state and instead gave much more land to the rising power of Turkey. There were several reasons for this. One was that Turkey had gone from being the broken remnant of the Ottoman Empire to something resurgent under Kemal Ataturk. His revolt in Turkey demonstrated the power of his support, including that of some Kurds who could not countenance the idea of a Kurdistan under the authority of the British. Ataturk, meanwhile, was no fan of the idea of an independent Kurdistan, standing in opposition to it because he claimed many of the same territories.

Sheik Mahmoud Barzanji's second revolt may have been another factor. Coming in 1922 when he returned from exile to regional governance, the attempt to proclaim the Kingdom of Kurdistan may have suggested to the British an unwillingness to work with their idea of how the future world order should go. It was also quickly clear that the kingdom did not have sufficient support to last, finally being defeated in 1924. They chose to ignore his claims while conceding those of Ataturk, giving way to the more powerful revolt that wasn't in their claimed territory in order to focus on the weaker one that was.

A third reason that came to be important after the treaty was the increasing belief that the newly formed Iraq might be a potential source of oil. It made the British unwilling to give up control of a region that might otherwise have been of only limited value to them, now knowing that it could give them a strategic advantage in the mechanised age.

In many ways, this revolt set the tone for others to follow: promises to the Kurds that never quite matched up to what they hoped for, and which were taken away when they rebelled at that fact; conflict against larger and usually more technologically advanced opponents; rebellions that worked as long as the world was distracted, but failed when a larger power gave Kurdistan its full attention; the opposition of regional powers scared of losing their own territories; and the exacerbating effects of oil wealth.

The result of the treaties was the creation of Iraq, and the installation of King Faisal by the British. It was a decision that would ultimately lead to more than a century of on and off war, genocide, and rebellion. Now, it is possible to suggest that some of this conflict might have occurred anyway, but there is also a case for saying that the least stable areas of the Middle East, and indeed the world, have been those with borders essentially imposed by the Great Powers of Europe and America in the wake of the world wars. The result of these essentially artificial countries has been instability, sometimes coming as ethnic groups with little in common have been forced together with one in an obvious position of authority, sometimes coming as the created governments have sought to defend their territories against those who believe in older and more obvious units. Sometimes, conflict has even been built into the new countries, as with the notion of Iraq being a "balance" to Iran: from the start, it was there to fight Iran periodically to stop it from growing too powerful.

Of course, we must not take the alternatives to this artificiality too far; the notion of "natural borders" is a fundamentally flawed, and often racially motivated, one. All borders are artificial human creations, produced through negotiation, warfare and the assertion of jurisdiction. Countries exist because humans join together to tell the story of their existence, not because they have any natural reason to do so. Even so, while there are no natural countries, there are obviously unnatural ones, and Iraq is one example.

The problems with Iraq made it obvious from the start that conflicts would continue within it. It was, and is, a country with multiple ethnic and religious groups jammed together, pressured by the surrounding countries and by the need for control over the country's oil resources. With those same pressures in place, it is hardly surprising that many of Kurdistan's rebellions have followed a similar pattern to those in 1919.

Some of the most important of those conflicts involved Masoud Barzani's father, Mullah Mustafa Barzani. In a parallel to Masoud Barzani's life, he was a young man fighting as a peshmerga in the 1919 rebellion, commanding some men, but yet to build up to a full position as a leader. Because of these parallels between their lives, and because his father's legacy seems to have shaped so much of Masoud Barzani's life, it is worth spending some time to understand Mullah Mustafa Barzani.

He was born in 1903, in a world that was still relatively conservative, relatively tribal, and relatively constrained within the Ottoman Empire. By sixteen, he was old enough to command men and take part in Sheik Mahmoud Barzanji's rebellion, learning many of the key lessons that would affect his life in the course of the 1920s, from the dangers of small scale asymmetrical warfare, to the likelihood of authorities lying to get their way, to the usefulness of retreating and regrouping, maintaining constant pressure towards a cause.

Perhaps this was the most important lesson that he learned, and one that Masoud Barzani would learn in turn later on: that change does not happen in one effort. It takes incremental steps, often involving rapid bursts forward, followed by pressure back that wipes out almost all of those achievements. It is a general but undulating trend, rather than a constant line of progress.

These were lessons that would come to be vital for Mullah Mustafa Barzani in the 1930s and 1940s. In 1929–30, he requested that the governor of Mosul replace British soldiers. The governor agreed to do so, but warned that this was likely to be a problem later on, perhaps knowing that Iraqi soldiers were likely to be even less sympathetic to the locals than the British soldiers who presently seemed like oppressors.

One effect of these Iraqi forces was that they jumped at any opportunity to clamp down on signs of rebellion. Where British forces had been content to sit in central locations, leaving the villages of the mountains in particular ignored, Iraqi soldiers were quick to use any hint of insurrection as an excuse to occupy villages, including those of the Barzanis.

At the time, one key Kurdish leader was Sheik Ahmad, who sought to bring together many of the Kurdish family and tribal groups into a broader organization founded on clear principles. He gained respect, sought to enhance the position of women, and to protect the environment at a time when neither was fashionable. Crucially, he began the process of moving Kurdistan away from tribal leadership and towards something broader.

None of this was acceptable to the Iraqi authorities under King Faisal. They sought Sheik Ahmad's arrest in the aftermath of one inter-tribal conflict, sending troops to apprehend him.

It may be that they thought that, in doing so, they were limiting the potential for rebellion down the line. After all, the 1930s were a time of rebellion elsewhere, with the Arrahat Rebellion in 1930–31 in Turkey leading to Sheik Ahmad taking in refugees displaced by the Turkish government. This may have made it look, to a suspicious government, as though he was preparing for his own rebellion.

Mullah Mustafa Barzani was intimately involved in all of this, experiencing the leadership of more than a small company of men for the first time. We know that he delivered the request to remove British forces from the area, and that he probably commanded many of the forces involved in the fights to unify various tribal structures. Certainly, he commanded one of the three sections of the three sections of the Barzani forces in 1932, when fighting broke out with the Iraqi government in earnest.

It seems likely in this conflict that he was able to use tactics and terrain to overcome superior numbers, although the exact numbers involved remain somewhat unclear, and perhaps do not matter. What matters more is that this was the first phase in which he was built up as a war leader, with the stories emphasising his ability to overcome seemingly difficult odds. There was an element of building him into a symbol of Kurdish unity and resistance, even then.

Those victories were impressive. Mullah Mustafa Barzani was working with a few hundred men, against probably more than a thousand of the enemy in some cases. In the Battle of Dola Vazhe, for example, we know that his forces succeeded in capturing around 250 men, and killing perhaps the same, with many running. It was a crucial battle, because it forced the government's forces to slow in their advance, coming to rely more upon attack from the air as they tried to batter the Barzani forces into submission.

Perhaps the reality of this bombardment was what formed the decision that came next, or perhaps it was the awareness that the government, with British support, could continue to send larger and larger forces until one succeeded. Finally, a suggestion of negotiation was sent out from the Barzani side, but Sheik Ahmad and his followers did not wait around to hear the answer, perhaps knowing that the British government would never be happy until they were all locked away.

To avoid this, they went into exile, and Mullah Mustafa Barzani went with them.

This initial withdrawal into Turkey was a well-planned thing, based on careful prior negotiations with the Turkish authorities. It allowed for only a relatively small proportion of those connected to the rebellion to travel there, but Mullah Mustafa Barzani was among their number. There was very little trust involved though, with the Turks requiring that they hand over their weaponry, and Sheik Ahmad's followers handing over only a small proportion of what they had.

At the border, the Turks changed the deal, allowing only Sheik Ahmad, Mullah Mustafa Barzani and a few other members of their families through, then moving them around from city to city in a way that seems to have been designed to prevent access to them by Kurdish forces, thus depriving them of their leaders. In 1933, Turkey went a step further, handing over Sheik Ahmad to the Iraqi authorities.

This left Mullah Mustafa Barzani with the choice of staying in Turkey, waiting to be handed over in turn, or returning to Iraq, where there would probably be more direct danger from the Iraqi government's forces. He chose Iraq, perhaps believing that it was an opportunity to at least have some control over whatever was going to happen next.

In returning, he and the others with him sought to avoid conflict for the time being, not striking at any government targets to avoid antagonising those who held Sheik Ahmad. At the same time, they did not believe the government's promises of an amnesty, and so remained in the mountains, away from their villages. It was a situation that couldn't last, and didn't. The Baghdad government used the promise of Sheik Ahmad to lure Mullah Mustafa Barzani to Mosul, and arrested him there.

He, his family and many of the others involved in the uprisings were taken to the south of Iraq, in the kind of internal exile that came to characterise many of the ethnically divided countries of the region. The theory was always that if someone was far from his or her own people, they could not do real damage or mount a meaningful insurrection.

Of course, this was not enough for the government, who viewed the rebellious Barzanis as traitors. In 1935, it held trials for many of those who had returned, and a number of them were executed. The government didn't feel as though it could do so with the leaders though, and both Mullah Mustafa Barzani and Sheik Ahmad survived. In 1936 there was an attempt to poison Mullah Mustafa Barzani more quietly, but following this, it seems that the government was content with the internal exile he was placed under, putting him and his family under house arrest in Sulaymaniyah.

It was not until 1943 that the Barzanis felt able to act again, with Mullah Mustafa Barzani taking advantage of Britain's commitment of resources elsewhere during the Second World War to slip out of Sulaymaniyah undetected. He left Iraq for Iran, trying to seek support there in a move reminiscent of his earlier passages across the border in the wake of rebellions. In this sense, it can be seen almost as a connecting phase between the defeat of the last rebellion and what followed.

What happened next was that Mullah Mustafa Barzani was able to raise thousands of soldiers; enough to be a significant force by the standards of Kurdistan at the time. He was to some extent a public and symbolic figure by this point, known for his earlier exploits, and people were willing to rally around his name as much as around the cause for which he stood. It is a symbolic value that we will see again in the course of his son's life.

Although the force was large by the standards of local ones, or even the uprisings that had gone before, it was still not on a scale that would allow it to meet the armies of a Western power, or even the Iraqi government, head on. This defined the character of the uprising that followed almost from the start. It meant that it could never involve more than hit and run tactics, and was likely to fail the moment one of those involved turned their full attention to it.

We can ask then why the rebellion in 1943 took place at all. Was it just a question of stubbornness, and an unwillingness to give up? There may have been an element of that, but there must have also have been glimmers of hope for Mullah Mustafa Barzani too, which suggested that it might be able to succeed if things went well. There was the wider context of the war, for example, which might have convinced him that, if he could establish enough of a territory for Kurdistan before it ended, he might be able to benefit from the same kind of rearranging of the map post war that had cost Kurdistan so dearly after the First World War. There was the possibility that small scale tactics might spark wider rebellion, swelling the scale of the forces available to him. There was even the possibility that, as caught up with the war as they were, he might have been able to force the British to the negotiating table, just so that they could free up resources for conflicts elsewhere.

There were multiple attacks on police stations, initially with relatively low bloodshed. There were small scale battles. There was support, but it was often quite passive. Ultimately, it seems that the aim was less to conquer and hold territory than it was simply to force the Iraqi government to the negotiating table. More importantly, it was about negotiating with the British who stood behind the Iraqi government. Mullah Mustafa Barzani knew that Baghdad stood opposed to everything he wanted, but that the British might give in to some of it, to allow them to focus on the wider war.

Those talks failed quickly. There are commentators who feel that the British wanted the return of violence all along, and were just using talks to gain time to bring their forces to bear. The defeat of Germany in 1945 certainly freed up resources for them to turn their attention back to Kurdistan. The refusal on both sides to settle for anything less than their full demands also contributed to the renewed violence.

The role of the Freedom Committee in the renewal of violence should not be underestimated. It was an attempt to bring together all the different strands of the struggle for an independent Kurdistan under one umbrella group. It was one of the first times that this had been done, bringing together the political and the military, moving to a more national perception of Kurdistan, rather than one based on particular tribes.

In the long term, it was a move that would change the face of Kurdish independence, putting it on a far broader footing, and potentially producing something that could form a nation. This very broadness made it more threatening, however, and prompted a renewal of violence from the British and the Iraqis.

The results were, initially, optimistic for the Barzani side. They won victories against larger forces in early attempts by the government to advance up the slopes of Mount Qalander and Bradost, and then ambushed government forces as they over-extended on the 5th of September at the gorge known as Maidan Morik.

Mullah Mustafa commanded the peshmerga of the Aqra front. He relied on the terrain of the mountains to encircle the advancing Iraqi forces as they sought to take villages, striking and then running, keeping just ahead of aerial bombardment from the British. The Kurdish forces used those opportunities to capture supplies, which served to fuel the conflict.

It couldn't last, though. In a classic case of winning battles but losing the war, Mullah Mustafa Barzani found legal and diplomatic pressure pulling his forces apart. The British persuaded his allies that the revolt was a Barzani matter, not a national one. The RAF applied pressure from the air too, inflicting casualties with no chance for the peshmerga forces to ever strike back.

Without the chance to move to a genuinely national war, the rebellion was stuck in an essentially defensive mode, losing slowly, forced to hit and run while the weather in autumn and winter steadily worsened. Mullah Mustafa Barzani was faced with a choice of continuing and seeing more deaths, or taking drastic action.

Yet again, he found himself forced to leave Iraq.

Writers have treated the Republic of Mahabad as everything from a successful dry run for Kurdistan as it stands to a historical oddity that failed to have real impact. It was not Mullah Mustafa Barzani's creation, although he came to play a key role in it. Instead, it came from the efforts of Qazi Muhammad, the Iranian lawyer and political leader responsible for the creation of the PDKI (Kurdish Democratic Party of Iran). He sought to carve out a territory under the protection of the Soviet Union rather than by declaring traditional lands independent unilaterally.

Qazi Muhammad was more urban than Mullah Mustafa Barzani, more connected to larger powers, and less military in approach, with less focus on rebellion. The Republic of Mahabad, meanwhile, was different in focus to the rebellions that had gone before, being more about creating something new than overthrowing an old order.

Qazi Muhammad and his supporters had been running Mahabad since 1941, and something resembling a free republic came into being in 1945. When Mullah Mustafa Barzani needed a place to flee to in the wake of his own revolt, it made obvious sense for him to take 3000 of his followers and head there, to the one place in the world that represented a free Kurdish state that was part of a larger burst of nationalist feeling at the end of World War Two. Azerbaijan chose that moment to try to gain independence from Iran as well, for example, and India would be free from British influence within just a few years.

Mullah Mustafa Barzani wanted a homeland for his people. The creation of the Mahabad Republic brought everything he had been trying to achieve for so long into existence, but not in the place he had thought it would come. The mass exodus that followed took immense and rapid planning.

Mullah Mustafa Barzani's impact on the Mahabad Republic is a matter for debate. He and his people were newcomers to the republic, but did play an important military role within it, and did become crucially connected to its leadership. This took time though, because Qazi Muhammad and his supporters seemed worried about giving a man so disliked by the British an obviously important place in it. Despite this, he played an important military and symbolic role.

The failure of the Mahabad Republic was largely a matter of the decisions of the greater powers around it. Following the Yalta agreement of 1946, the Soviet Union withdrew its support, leaving the way free for Iran to invade. Once more, Mullah Mustafa Barzani found a force of a few thousand men facing the armies of a much bigger nation. Once more, victory was impossible, so that it became inevitable that the Mahabad Republic would collapse.

We can ask how much the Mahabad Republic achieved, or whether Mullah Mustafa Barzani really intended to stay there permanently. Those are questions that are addressed elsewhere, but for now, the Mahabad Republic is vitally important, because it was the place where Masoud Barzani was born.

CHAPTER TWO

Childhood

WHY DO WE discuss the childhoods of great men? The important things that they do invariably come as adults, and often as older adults. Yet people continue to discuss their childhoods as if searching for some sign of the man to come. Perhaps it is because we instinctively search for the things that happened to make them into who they would become. Perhaps it is because we feel that if we can identify those elements, we might be able to spot those who will be great in the future.

Of course, there are elements of caution needed in that. It is a truism in history that if you go looking for something, you will probably find it, because the sheer breadth of events in most periods, even most lives, allows for selections of events to fit almost any narrative. We find signs of who men become precisely *because* we go looking for them. This is not to deny the events themselves, but simply to note that out of all the events of a childhood, we will inevitably focus on those that most

23

relate to the person someone became, rejecting others. But if we think about it, would not many of the same experiences be found in other people who did not achieve as much? Indeed, in looking back at a great person's childhood to suggest a kind of inevitability to the ascent, we risk accidentally insulting them. We take away some of the agency they exercised in becoming who they did.

In Masoud Barzani's case, though, there is some value to be had in looking at his childhood, for a number of reasons. First, even from an early age, he was used on a symbolic level within the cause of Kurdish independence. His family background, moreover, meant that from the earliest age, he knew that he would be involved in that cause on some level. It was a childhood, in many ways, designed with who he would become in mind.

Second, his childhood involved a number of very unusual circumstances, brought about by the consequences of the fight for independence. His father's actions in previous uprisings had knock on effects on Masoud Barzani's childhood, helping to shape the man he would become, or at least limiting his alternative options. In this sense, his childhood is interesting because it was different from many of the other childhoods around the world.

Thirdly, it is useful to consider Masoud Barzani's childhood because of just how early he became involved in the cause. By most reckonings he would still have been a child at that point, and it is vital to understand his childhood if we are to understand his first taste of the cause of independence that would come to define his life.

Birth

Masoud Barzani was born on the 16th of August 1946 in the Mahabad Republic. The story is that when he was born, he was wrapped in the republic's flag, and while this may seem like the kind of detail that could have been invented afterwards, there are obvious reasons why it might be true:

One is that this was a birth taking place in a newly independent state, and it makes sense that Masoud Barzani's parents would want to reinforce the importance of that. It makes sense that his father, in particular, would want this, given Mulluh Mustafa Barzani's commitment to the cause of Kurdish independence.

Another is that the Barzani family was becoming very aware of the power of symbolism at that point. In the 1943 rebellion and before, there had not been sufficient men to truly hope to hold territory against the larger forces of the government for long. The best that could be hoped for was to achieve sufficient success for the idea of Kurdistan to spread.

This has long been one of the core elements of asymmetrical warfare: that the aims are not necessarily physical, but may sometimes be symbolic; that sometimes the purpose of attacks or other actions is to be seen, or even to draw retaliation, so that it may draw others towards a cause.

Indeed, we can say that one of the elements that has helped successive members of the Barzani family to do so much for the cause of Kurdish independence is their awareness of the power of symbolism, and their ability to weave the disparate elements of Kurdish nationalism together into one coherent story that can attract support. Sheik Ahmad brought people together with common principles, Mullah Mustafa Barzani did it with a broader sense of Kurdistan as a country, and Masoud Barzani would come to expand this to provide a sense of what Kurdistan is today.

It is probably only right, therefore, that he was wrapped in the flag when he was born. It showed Masoud Barzani what his life was meant to be, and the cause to which it was supposed to be dedicated. It also said to him, quite clearly, that he was Kurdish, not 'Iraqi', not part of a country made up by the British to suit their oil and security interests.

It is also an important moment in Masoud Barzani's life, not in the sense that he had any control over it, because he didn't, but in terms of what it says about him being woven into the narratives constructed around the Barzanis, around Kurdistan, and around the interaction between the two. The Barzanis have been good at understanding that narrative, and at shaping it in a way that put them at its heart. It was a moment designed to symbolise patriotism, but it was also one designed to suggest to the watching Kurdish audience that here was a child who would have a significant role to play in the fortunes of Kurdistan.

We now know that was true, of course, although there is a self-fulfilling element to the prediction. The very act of using Masoud Barzani's birth as a symbol of rebellion raised him up, providing the first of very many steps that would push him towards being a leader. In that sense, his story is as much about the power of narrative within Kurdistan and who controls it as it is about the physical conflicts that have marked his life.

The Flight from Mahabad

Of course, for a time after his birth, it is hard to tell much of Masoud Barzani's story beyond the general history of the time. Children do not generally make such waves on the international stage that they are reported in history. Beyond the small symbolic moment around his birth, Masoud Barzani disappears from sight at this point, eclipsed by the events surrounding him and by the actions of his father. Even so, it is interesting to think of what it must have been like for a baby, and then a young boy, caught up in these events, seeing these things first-hand in the years that we know shape so much of who we are.

The most immediate event following Masoud Barzani's birth was the escape of the Barzanis from the failing Republic of Mahabad. While it had briefly shown that an independent Kurdish state run along (for the time) modern political lines was possible, following the 1946 Yalta agreement it was only a matter of time before it was crushed. As happened so often in his life Mullah Mustafa Barzani saw the oncoming storm and knew that he had to evacuate his people or watch them be slaughtered.

Perhaps the birth of Masoud Barzani even played a role in that decision. It is not inconceivable that a new father would want to protect his child rather than risking the uncertainties of battle. At the same time though, retreating to fight another day was a key tactic that had already served Mullah Mustafa Barzani well in his career as both a peshmerga and a leader. It seems likely that he would have adopted the same strategy regardless, and that the birth of his son merely made it more pressing that he do so.

There was an initial period of delay and negotiation with the Iranian commander. He clearly made a distinction between the Barzanis and the other inhabitants of the republic, perhaps because they had arrived en masse to join it, and perhaps also because they had been leaving one potentially violent situation when they did so. The commander was probably aware of the possibility of avoiding conflict with a potentially very dangerous armed force, and saw the opportunity to take the last of the Mahabad Republic's defences from it. The Iranian government made offers of farmland to the Barzanis, clearly trying to persuade them away from their involvement in the republic. As had happened in other, similar situations though, the negotiations drew out. Mullah Mustafa Barzani sought more time, saying that he needed to consult with his brother, Sheik Ahmad, before he could make any decision. This may even have been true, although by this point, Mullah Mustafa Barzani was very much the main military decision maker for the Barzanis.

The Iranian commander agreed to this time to consult, which both gave Mullah Mustafa Barzani a way to return safely to his people and bought him time in which to act. The commander's reason for agreeing was probably a desire to avoid direct conflict with a hardened guerrilla force, rather than any sense of doing the right thing, but the reasoning is immaterial. What matters is that Mullah Mustafa Barzani had gained a little time in which to act.

He knew that he could not return to Iraq, because he was a wanted man, and the act of escape into voluntary exile had only made it worse. He knew that he could not accept the Iranian

offer, either. Partly, this was because of his genuine commitment to the idea of an independent Kurdistan, which would
inevitably put him at odds with the Iranians, and partly, it
was because he had no reason to believe that they would keep
up their end of the bargain. As would be seen again and again
around the world, it was all too easy for leaders to pretend
to make concessions, only to go back on them or even seek
to kill those they had supposedly made peace with. The best
he could hope for in that scenario was to be under a form of
house arrest. The worst would be to be murdered.

It was decided that the majority of the Barzanis would
be safest returning to Iraq, so on the 19th of April 1947,
the Barzanis crossed the border from Iran back into Iraq.
Mullah Mustafa Barzani knew that he couldn't stay though,
because that would attract too much attention from the Iraqi
government. The march of the 500 that followed has become
famous in Kurdistan. He and 500 of those most at risk of
being killed by the government made a truly perilous march
over the mountains in poor weather, and with opposition
from Iranian forces. They pushed into Azerbaijan and then,
later, found themselves moved to Uzbekistan. It was a march
that forged links between Mullah Mustafa Barzani and the
Soviet Union, and saw him becoming a commander in one
of their divisions.

It was also a move that separated him from his new born
son. Masoud Barzani was too young to be taken on such a
dangerous journey, and in any case, there was no price on his
head yet. There was no reason for he and the rest of Mullah
Mustafa Barzani's family to march, and every reason for them

not to. Not going effectively separated them from the efforts of Mullah Mustafa Barzani, limiting the scope for retaliation. The safest thing for them at that time was to return to Iraq and settle there peacefully, giving the government no reason to believe that they posed a threat.

How hard must that decision to separate have been, not knowing if they would ever see one another again? Today, it seems improbable, even unkind, yet it probably was the kindest thing in the circumstances. Mullah Mustafa Barzani would have attracted enemies, so he had to leave. His family could not make the journey, so they had to stay and thrive. It is the kind of decision that families are forced into making even today, in a world where cruelty and violence can often tear them apart. Even when separations are not permanent, there are many situations where one parent is forced to go away to work far from home, while another is left to bring up a family essentially alone.

I have explored the journey of the 500 and its consequences elsewhere. For now, it is more relevant to keep our focus with those left behind, who had to try to find a life in Iraq after those they loved had set out, on a march that meant they would not be seen again for a decade.

Early Years

As noted before, we look at the childhoods of great men in the expectation, even the hope, that we will find evidence of the men they would eventually become. We do this partly because we want to confirm to ourselves that this is how the world works, partly because we want to believe in the inevitability of their success, and partly because we want to have those consistent markers with which to spot potential greatness in those around us, even in ourselves.

The truth is that it is far more complicated than that. An individual may show early signs of particular character traits or abilities, but there are many people with those traits who will not achieve a similar level of success, or affect the world in the same ways. Someone must have the right circumstances around them, the right opportunities to act, and the right support to fulfil a potential that then seems as if it couldn't have turned out any other way. It is easy to look back along the line of a life and pick out traits that we believe brought someone success (usually traits that accord with our own view of the world). It is much harder to look at a pool of individuals and know which of them are likely to have success.

It is at least as hard, even impossible, to pick out the life of a single child in the 1940s and 1950s in Iraq. In this, they suffer the fate of most of the people who have ever lived in history: their actions are not recorded. There is a reason that work on the past used to focus on great figures: it was easier to produce, because there were biographies and papers, notes about their actions and even statues. As time has gone on, the field of view of history has expanded somewhat, Even today, in a world of social media and parents taking constant photographs of their children, it would be hard, but in a space where children were not treated in this way, and where attention flowed only from the actions of their parents, it is almost impossible.

We can say a few general things, of course. We know that the returning men, women and children were met with deep suspicion by the authorities, and many were resettled in such a way that it would be hard for them to take up arms again in the future. The notion was that if families were cut off from contact with their native regions, then they would not be connected into the networks of support that produced uprisings. It is a tactic with a long history in Iraq, and which to some extent has worked, as it has always been a necessary first step for any uprising for the leaders to escape their confinement and cross the country to meet up with their supporters.

As a result, many of the families of the returning fighters found themselves relocated to areas such as Sulaymaniyah, where they were far from traditionally Barzani centres of influence. It is hard to say to what extent this would have disrupted Masoud Barzani's early life though, since much of it seems to have been spent between a mixture of Iraq and Iran. We know that he was eventually able to complete high school in Iran, and that his early life was probably disrupted repeatedly, but that he was at least able to go to school there.

He had many brothers, since Mustafa Barzani had ten sons. Masoud Barzani was not the oldest of them, with the result that there was probably never a sense of him being groomed for leadership in the way that we might believe. Indeed, there couldn't have been, when the authorities would have been looking out for any indication that such a thing was the case, and would have sought to clamp down on it. In that sense, the more normal his childhood could be, the safer he was.

In general, though, the most that we can say of Masoud Barzani's childhood is that much of it was fairly normal for one of the sons of an important family. He would have done all of the things that children did, and may even have felt in that phase that nothing very special was going to happen in his life. After all, his father's efforts to bring about an independent Kurdistan had failed, and there was no reason to suspect that anything was going to change in the near future. Perhaps we can posit a phase in which it must have seemed possible to Masoud Barzani that he would have a different kind of life.

What might that life have been? He was educated, and from a well-known family, so it seems likely that there would still have been some involvement in government or officialdom. Perhaps that thought, though, is simply that the pull of what is is so strong that it influences thoughts of what might have been. It is easy to think of things turning out this way anyway, of the sheer force of the former president being enough to bring about the same end. In that, there are two elements at play: one is a recognition we must all make that our lives are subject to complex series of decisions by others. So many things had to happen in exactly the right places for things to turn out as they did that Masoud Barzani's role in Kurdistan was anything but inevitable.

The other runs in the opposite direction, which is the power of the narrative the Barzanis have consistently told, weaving them and the cause of independence together. This narrative gave Masoud Barzani a lot of authority as he joined the movement, and made it natural that he should move up the ranks under the guidance of his family.

This does not detract from Masoud Barzani's achievements; if anything, it amplifies them, because it reminds us of all the ways that things could have turned out differently. A series of key events turned a relatively ordinary childhood into a life that was dedicated to independence. One of the most crucial was the revolution of 1958.

1958

1958 marked two important events that changed the course of Masoud Barzani's life, effectively marking the beginning of the end for his childhood as he had known it before. Indeed, they changed the course of events for the whole of Iraq and Kurdistan.

The first of these was the coup d'etat within Baghdad of the 14th of July, which saw the overthrow of Iraq's then ruling family. It involved the deaths of King Faisal II, his heir, and the prime minister. The circumstances leading up to the revolution are complex, involving broad pressures that had been building within Iraq for some considerable time.

The first element was antipathy towards the continuing influence of the British within Iraq, fuelled by a sense of Arab nationalism. Almost since the inception of the country, Britain had run Iraq essentially as a vassal state, installing a king who would give them preferential treatment, and supporting their companies to extract Iraq's natural resources. In return, their military support helped to maintain the control of the Iraqi royal family, as we saw in the previous chapter, where RAF bombing was one of the major contributing factors to the failure of Kurdistan's rebellions.

In part, the very desire to build up a sense of Iraq as a country contributed to this anti-British feeling. While Iraq was a divided place, there was no coherent body to revolt. When there was more a sense of it as a place, there was an opportunity for nationalism to build up, centred on an Arab ethnic identity. At the same time, the efforts to impose control in a new country forced a backlash from its inhabitants. There is a certain irony to this, given the ways Baghdad has since tried to stop Kurdish attempts at independence since. Perhaps that is because it is aware of how easily nationalist feelings can turn into more. Certainly, at the time, it helped to create the conditions where a revolution might happen.

The things that turned it into a reality were more short term though, with a combination of economic hardship and unpopular political agreements. Economically, Iraq had been suffering since the end of World War Two, falling into a recession and then a depression. This necessitated greater exploitation of Iraq's oil resources in order to offset the economic damage, which was unpopular because it essentially meant Britain taking more and more of Iraq's natural wealth, this highlighting the already existing inequalities.

The political decisions included, notably, the Baghdad Pact with Iran, Turkey and Pakistan, tying Iraq to countries that it had existing grievances with. The Suez Canal crisis of 1956 worsened things, while the real tipping point came in 1958, when the British and French invaded Egypt to try to regain control, and Iraq found itself forced to support the British. Egypt and Syria then entered into the UAR pact, supporting one another based on pan-Arabism. Iraq didn't wish to join this pact, but instead formed one with Jordan to try to balance it. The result of all these pressures was revolution, aimed at removing all British and US influence from Iraq.

Like many revolutions, it was both a sudden thing and a thing that had obviously, in retrospect, been building up for some time. It meant that those living in Iraq or Kurdistan would have already formed positions or opinions on what was happening.

The revolution must have been disruptive in general terms for Masoud Barzani, but in a lot of ways he was probably as insulated from it as any twelve-year-old might have been. It did have one immediate impact on his life, though, because the newly founded Republic of General Abdulkarim Qasim welcomed Mustafa Barzani and his followers back to Iraq from their exile in the USSR.

What must it have been like for Masoud Barzani to be reunited with his father after so long apart? We can assume that there would not have been the immediate connection that a movie might assume, and that it would have taken time for things to settle into a normal routine. Masoud Barzani and his father would have needed time in which to build a normal father-son relationship with one another, because the last time they had met, Masoud Barzani was no more than a baby, while Mullah Mustafa Barzani had yet to be shaped by his time in the USSR.

The later evidence seems to suggest that they *did* form a good relationship, though. After all, Masoud Barzani effectively became his father's deputy in most things in later life, and acted on his authority in much the same way that his father had earlier acted using Sheik Ahmad's name. Perhaps this was because, at the time, father-son relations were expected to be a certain way, rather than being built on a close, personal knowledge of the other in a way that we might expect today. Perhaps it was because the absence formed part of a wider swathe of them.

Even so, we must ask whether there would have been any sense of abandonment present in that moment of return. Mullah Mustafa Barzani might have had no choice about his exile, but even so, it must have seemed strange to his son to have him simply walking back into their lives in 1958, no matter how joyous the occasion otherwise was.

1958, then, probably marked the beginning of a kind of normal family life for Masoud Barzani, but also the disruption of the status quo. That didn't just come through the return of his father, but also through his father's quick reinvolvement in the politics of Iraq, and in the cause of independence from it. It meant that Masoud Barzani would start to see first-hand what that cause involved, but it also meant that any hint that he might have gone from an ordinary childhood to an ordinary life started to fade. His father's return marked the moment when Masoud Barzani started to be pulled into the cause of independence as something other than just a passive spectator, and so we must turn to the first active choice he made in that direction: becoming a peshmerga.

Becoming a Peshmerga

Masoud Barzani became a Peshmerga in 1963. At that stage, he was not a leader, although he would soon become one. We can only speculate on what that would have been like in those first days for him, asking whether it would have been the same for him as it would have been for every other peshmerga at the time. We must also ask another question, which is why it was that year in particular.

I want to address each of those things in turn.

It seems likely that much of Masoud Barzani's experience of becoming a peshmerga would have been typical. Given the dangers involved, there was no room for special treatment. He would have had to learn the skills involved alongside older and more experienced men. Given his later history, it seems that he learned those lessons well.

What would those lessons have included? To answer that, we must understand more about the nature of the peshmerga at the time. We know that they had been relatively informal troops, joining up as needed in the rebellions that had previously occurred. This was generally acceptable, as the people within individual, isolated villages already had a good knowledge of how to use rifles and other small arms to hunt, how to survive within the mountains and how to stay quiet. The peshmerga were dangerous because those skills were so ingrained in the Kurdish way of life, rather than because they were added afterwards.

Yet we know that Mullah Mustafa Barzani's return meant some changes for the peshmerga forces. In his time in the Soviet Union, he had been exposed to other methods of warfare, to more formal training in tactics and strategy, and to weapon systems beyond those that had previously been available to peshmerga forces. We know, for example, that he brought greater organisation to Kurdistan's fighting forces, with clearer lines of command and communication, and that he helped to set out a measure of the training in unconventional warfare that helped to push the peshmerga in the direction of being one of the foremost small unit forces available.

Even if Masoud Barzani had not been his son, he would have joined the peshmerga at just the right moment to receive the benefits of this greater organisation. It is likely that he received more in the way of formal training than preceding generations of fighters because of that timing, gaining the benefit of tactics and knowledge that came back with his father from his time in exile.

Because Mullah Mustafa Barzani was his father, though, it also seems likely that Masoud Barzani would have benefited from addition instruction. Just his father's stories of his time fighting would have contained lessons that most boys his age would never have had a chance to learn. He would have learned about the arts of leadership both through example and direct instruction, might well have been privy to information kept confidential from others, and would certainly have been in a better position than most to understand the political context of the actions taken by his family.

Expectations

Throughout his life, Masoud Barzani has been wrapped up in the narrative that the Barzanis have constructed around independence. They have been aware that independence and sovereignty, the desire to fight against repressive authority and the desire for statehood are potentially complex ideas, whose nuanced arguments can sometimes lose the attention of the population at large, or be insufficient to spark an emotional response. They have always understood that it is only by constructing a coherent narrative around independence that they are able to persuade people to rise up and seek greater control over their region.

The Barzanis have long woven themselves into this narrative, stressing their commitment to the cause of independence and the role of key members of their family as leaders. By doing so, they have consistently put themselves in a position to help drive the cause of independence forward, and to direct some of the activities involved. It is a position forged out of their readiness to act to defend Kurdistan against those outside forces that might try to impose control on it against the will of its population.

It also means that the Barzani name comes with at least some expectations, so we must assess what those expectations meant for Masoud Barzani as he was growing up.

First, what would those expectations have been? Generally, the connection to the Barzani name has carried with it an expectation of connection to the cause of independence, and this was particularly true in the period when Masoud Barzani was growing up. This connection had been explicitly reinforced by his father through wrapping him in the flag when he was born, and was implicit in his return. It is notable that the transformation of Masoud Barzani's life to become a peshmerga only happened after his father came back from the USSR. This may have been simply a function of his age at the time, since he was finally growing old enough to take part in the wider cause, but may also have been strongly connected to the role of his father as a point of inspiration and a source of expectations. Through much of his life, we can see Masoud Barzani as striving to live up to the example set by his father, even as he started to move in a somewhat different, more political, direction.

CHAPTER THREE

Rising to Leadership

HOW DID MASOUD BARZANI go from a peshmerga to the leader of Kurdistan's largest political party? It was not a quick process, and was one that took at least a couple of decades to occur. It began with the simplest levels of leadership, as he gained the experience necessary to lead other peshmerga in the field. This might not seem like much, but it was possibly, in many ways, the most important step. The point at which he started to command others was the first at which he had to show his own talents, rather than relying on his family connections or any outside sense of who he was.

Yet those connections *were* crucial, because as early as sixteen, his father had him involved in the political sphere alongside him, serving as an aide, a messenger, a confidante and a second pair of eyes. The acceleration to these positions came from forces that will be familiar to any student of Kurdistan: the need to rely on family for support in the face of stressful and dangerous times.

Masoud Barzani became a peshmerga in 1963, but that was also the year of the military uprising in Iraq. The new rulers of Iraq had little trust in the KDP, led by Mustafa Barzani, but in the initial phase, both factions were busier with their own internal struggles than with the potential for independence. Masoud Barzani's father sought to consolidate his place within the party. He made sure that its structures were consistent, but also fought off potential rivals for the leadership (leading to the eventual split with the PUK). It is possibly the internal nature of some of these early conflicts that prompted him to make so much use of his sons.

It is here that we must mention Masoud Barzani's brother, Idris Barzani. Perhaps if things had turned out differently, it might have been his history that we were tracing now, and without his death in his forties in 1987, it seems certain that he would have played some key role within Kurdistan and the KDP. He and Masoud Barzani were crucial extensions of their father's efforts in this period, often working together, but also acting independently where needed. In 1964, for example, it was Idris Barzani who did much of the work of driving Jalal Talabani's faction out of the KDP, and eventually over the border into Iran.

In this phase, aside from moments such as this, it is sometimes hard to pick out individual actions of Masoud or Idris Barzani from those of their father. This is natural; Mullah Mustafa Barzani was a great, charismatic leader at the time, and the attention was naturally on him. His sons, meanwhile, would often have seemed like aides to those around him. Even towards the end of his life, in the period he spent in America, there are reports that he went everywhere with a number of family members, in a way that the Americans often had trouble understanding, seeing it as typical 'strongman dictator' behaviour, rather than the natural extension of not being able to trust anyone else.

Because of this core of family, and because of the relatively stable situation within the party, by 1965, Mustafa Barzani felt able to demand independence from the new government of Iraq. It reacted with a hostility that will be a familiar pattern throughout this book, with almost a hundred thousand Iraqi soldiers being deployed to put down what it saw as an insurrection. As both one of his father's closest aides and a peshmerga, Masoud Barzani was embroiled in this fighting, during which supplies over the Iranian border meant that the peshmerga were able to keep fighting despite the advance from the south, with the Iraqi army unable to defeat them conclusively in terrain that favoured them and with the approach of winter favouring those who both knew the terrain and were used to surviving in it. It meant that, although the government had superior numbers, they were not able to overwhelm the KDP's forces as they might have hoped. They even found themselves having to make a deal with Talabani's forces, hoping for their help in dealing with the shared foe of the KDP.

This would not have been the first fighting that Masoud Barzani had faced, but it would have been the most serious to date, with significant enemy forces, and only the advantages of asymmetrical warfare to keep him and those men he commanded safe. The war dragged on into the winter, but there must have been a brief moment of hope for its cessation when

President Arif of Iraq died in April 1966. Perhaps Masoud Barzani was one of those who hoped that a change in government might bring a change in attitude towards the Kurds, or perhaps he was one of those who saw that the desire of the Iraqi government to hang on to the region went far beyond one man. In the absence of specific evidence, we cannot say which, but events since have certainly proved the latter to be true.

In this case, the new president, and brother of the old president, Abdul Rahman Arif, sought not just to continue the conflict, but to escalate it in an effort to finish it quickly. The divisions of the Iraqi army forced their way forward. We know in this period that the peshmerga drew on their existing experience of fighting larger forces. It also seems that they had at least some military advisors from Israel, which also had experience of winning against such larger forces, and which saw Kurdistan as an ally, able to tie up Iraqi forces so that they would not be able to attack it. Masoud Barzani is likely to have been present at some of the planning meetings where the decisions were made, and to have at least learned the lessons involved, perhaps even contributed to those plans.

The plans were initially simple: defences were constructed, designed to slow and hold back the Iraqi army. At the same time though, the peshmerga understood the inevitability of those defences being breached, so Mullah Mustafa Barzani and those around him sought to take advantage of the advance that would follow, luring Iraqi divisions forward onto the slopes of Mount Handrin and almost completely destroying that division in a demonstration of superior tactics that would slow the course of the war and prevent the destruction of Kurdistan's forces.

The conflict continued, however, and in 1967, the changing nature of it, and the importance of intelligence to it, led to Masoud Barzani getting what was then his most important role to date, as one of those who helped to found the intelligence service of the KDP: the Parastin Agency.

It is hard to overestimate just how important this intelligence agency has been to the KDP, and to Kurdistan in general. In any conflict fought in guerrilla fashion, and in a push for independence from a larger and more powerful force more generally, it is vital to have intelligence about an opponent's likely actions, while guarding against the threats of infiltration, sudden attacks, or betrayal. The Parastin Agency initially sought to provide information that would prove to be of use in the ongoing conflict with Baghadad, but also sought to ensure the unity of Kurdistan's forces in a period when it seemed that Baghdad was determined to use dissident Kurdish factions against the KDP.

To understand how important a move the founding of this intelligence agency was, it is worth remembering that the PUK's equivalent, the Zanyari Agency, was not founded until 1991. In this, Masoud Barzani was a trailblazer within Kurdistan, understanding that warfare, and even government, under such difficult conditions came down to more than those things done openly. The functioning of the Parastin may well explain why Kurdistan has been able to avoid many of the collapses and coups that have afflicted surrounding regions, even Iraq.

Indeed, such a coup in Iraq took place in the year after the Parastin's founding, 1968. The Ba'athist elements in Iraq took full control, rather than being just minor partners in the government. The removal of Abdul Rahman Arif as president did not initially halt the conflict with Kurdistan, however, but it did remove at least one obstacle to the stopping of the war, and would eventually result in peace, in 1970.

Before that, however, Masoud Barzani was involved in other matters. In 1969, following the Six Day War with Israel, Baghdad started hunting down and persecuting what was by then its small remaining Jewish community, accusing them of being traitors. Many Jews had already left Iraq, emigrating to Israel following its inception as a modern state, but the new round of attacks and government sanctioned murders led to more seeking to flee. We know from the accounts of those at the time that Masoud Barzani was a part of the efforts that led to more than a thousand people being smuggled through Kurdistan to safety, driving some of the vehicles involved himself. Kurdistan has often felt that it has shared more in common with its Jewish neighbours than with those Arab nations who have oppressed its people and subjected them to violence, so it is hardly surprising that Masoud Barzani and the KDP would wish to help. Arguably, doing so also helped to maintain relationships that would prove invaluable throughout Masoud Barzani's career.

Perhaps his successes in helping to organise this evacuation also played a part in ensuring that he was selected for his next important role: as one of the key negotiators involved in the 1970 peace settlement with Baghdad. While today, it may seem that it was a peace settlement that did not result in true independence, and that in some ways it paved the way for conflicts to come, we must also say that it was vital, because it produced the boundaries of an autonomous Kurdistan, enshrining the idea of it within not just the imagination, but in Iraqi law as well.

In this, Masoud Barzani helped to bring about some of the first formal recognition of a distinct Kurdish area, and of the principle of autonomy from Baghdad. It was a moment that helped to legitimise the foundations of the current Kurdistan, and that has also served as a basis from which to imagine the idea of a more fully independent state. It could be argued that without the settlement of 1970, and without Masoud Barzani's role in helping to bring it about, there would have been no referendum in 2017, no push towards independence. Two moments, almost fifty years apart, yet both aiming towards broadly the same ends, and encompassing at least a broadly similar region in spite of the 1970 settlement's more restricted region.

Being a negotiator in 1970 did more than to help establish the idea of a Kurdistan in northern Iraq as autonomous, however. It also had profound effects for Masoud Barzani's life to come. While he and his brother Idris Barzani had long been earmarked as key figures for the future within the KDP, the negotiations helped to announce Masoud Barzani to the wider stage. With his name out there, it made it more obvious that he would play a key part in future relations between Kurdistan and Baghdad, building his experience of statesmanship while exposing others to the idea that he should be someone to talk with about governmental matters. In some ways, it was the same strategy that Sheik Ahmad used with Mullah Mustafa

Barzani in earlier conflicts with the British, sending him in his stead, both so that there would always be an excuse to go back to ask for final confirmation of a position and so that it would establish the next leader in line.

How successful were the negotiations? The March 11th agreement of 1970 allowed for a semi-autonomous Kurdistan region, but that region was smaller than the one today, and more limited in its autonomy. It was certainly not the independent state that was, and is, Kurdistan's final aim. In that sense, we can say that Masoud Barzani and the other negotiators did not achieve all that they might have wished to achieve. Yet we can also say that they probably achieved more in the direction of independence than anyone within Iraq had in the past. They also achieved about as much as could realistically be expected, given that the objectives of the Baghdad negotiators were to maintain Iraq's territorial integrity.

Partly in recognition of the scale of this success, and partly as a continuation of his progress towards leadership, 1970 also saw Masoud Barzani elected to the KDP's central committee for the first time, while he would also join other groups within it. The result of this was that he began to be a true part of the decision making processes of the party, moving from someone who simply carried out his father's orders to someone who helped to shape the KDP's positions on everything from domestic policy to approaches to independence. In this sense, 1970 represents the first point where we can see Masoud Barzani acting of his own accord, rather than simply tracing his father's actions and assuming that he was there beside him.

Of course, he continued to be by his father's side, and we must not overstate the extent of this separate identity. Part of the point was that Masoud Barzani was close to and trusted by Mullah Mustafa Barzani, with the result that he continued to work alongside him within the KDP, even as things started to go wrong with the 1970 agreement.

The problem with that agreement was not a failure by the negotiators, but something more fundamental built into the positions of the two sides. Kurdistan continued to want full independence, while Baghdad wanted Iraq to be a coordinated whole, run from Baghdad. In that sense, the 1970 agreement suited neither. Worse, each side viewed the agreement differently. For Baghdad, the March 11th agreement was meant to be a final settlement of the 'Kurdish question', a position that would never change, except perhaps to make the Kurds more integrated in a newly nationalistic Iraq. It was a way to shut up a rebellious faction, but not one that had to be implemented in full. For Kurdistan, however, it is clear that the same agreement represented only a staging post from which to push on to more. The two positions were fundamentally incompatible, with the result that further conflict was only a matter of time.

Perhaps if the agreement had been implemented, it would have slowed the slide into conflict, but it was not. In one sense, perhaps Masoud Barzani and the others had negotiated too well: they had gained agreement to things that the Iraqi government quickly regretted and did not feel that it could give them. Making the agreement bought Baghdad a few years, but the failure to implement it meant a renewal of violence in 1974. The conflict of 1974–5 was one that Masoud Barzani, as a peshmerga, was heavily involved in, although as with so many other events of the period, his actions are hard to trace in the shadow of his father's. We can say that he was involved in the fighting, which was hard going against an Iraqi army that remained superior in terms of heavy armaments. Worse, this conflict quickly turned into a straight ahead war, rather than the guerrilla conflict that had gone before. It meant that the Kurdish forces were forced to rely on support from Iran in pursuing their side of the war, gaining supplies from them in a way that was often backed by the CIA.

This makes sense when we understand that most of the Iran-Iraq tensions of the period served as a kind of proxy war between the USA and USSR, with each supporting different sides in the Middle East in an effort to gain control in a region where they did not feel that they could act directly. It is the kind of conflict that still has echoes today in Syria. In 1974–5, though, it meant guns paid for with US money going through Iran to find their way to the Kurdish forces, in the days before the Iranian revolution when the US still backed Iran in the region.

That could only last so long, though, and Masoud Barzani was to have one of his first tastes of abandonment by an international backer in the way that his father had already experienced in Mahabad. Iran and Iraq signed the Algiers Accords with the brokering of the USA, which felt that it was gaining an overall position as a trusted partner of both by doing so. That it involved the abandonment of Kurdistan's forces did not matter to it. It was a lesson that Masoud Barzani would see again and again through his life.

For now, it meant the collapse of the attempted revolution, with Iraqi armour now free to move forward to crush the Kurdish forces. Mullah Mustafa Barzani was forced to leave Kurdistan for America, and would not see it again during his lifetime. Masoud Barzani would ultimately go with him, along with his brother Idris, but not before they had helped to establish the Provisional Leadership, dedicated to continuing the fight for independence. This body was particularly important, as it sought to counter the effects of Saddam's programme to regain control of Kurdistan and turn it into an Iraqi, Arab, region. These policies included the destruction of villages, the forced migration of Kurdish families within Iraq, effectively seeking to break up any sense of community, and the equally forced resettlement of Arab families into formerly Kurdish areas such as Kirkuk. Without some organisation dedicated to continuing the fight, it seems likely that Kurdistan as an idea might have been destroyed in that phase.

In the next few years, Masoud Barzani spent much of his time with his father in America, joining him some time after his arrival. It seems that period was anything but a comfortable one, and not just because Mullah Mustafa Barzani was being treated for inoperable cancer. The CIA watched their every move, ostensibly as their hosts in the country but more realistically as a way to limit what they were able to say to figures of authority or the press about what had happened back in Kurdistan. While Masoud Barzani was involved in attempts to get to Washington to allow his father to tell his story, the Americans ensured that turned into no more than a sightseeing trip, refusing to stop anywhere they might be able to speak to those in authority. The truth was that many of those in authority weren't interested in listening.

They returned Mustafa Barzani and those around him to Iran, briefly, in Iran, many of those who had fought were caught in camps that were ostensibly refugee camps but which were heavily guarded and there to prevent any shift of the movement for independence northward. There was fighting, meanwhile, with PUK factions, which complicated any attempt to reorganise and renew the movement in the south. In 1976, Mullah Mustafa Barzani was allowed to return to the USA for treatment, his son going with him. Although he was able to tell his story to the press and to limited government hearings, he was able to take no further major actions on the international stage before his death in 1979.

Masoud Barzani, however, continued to undertake journeys both on behalf of his father and for Kurdistan's cause more generally. One crucial one came at the start of 1979, when he met with officials working for Imam Khomeini of Iran, in order to coordinate Kurdish efforts with the wider revolt against the regime of the Shah there. The meeting took place in Paris, and from there, he sought to make his way back towards Iraq, moving across Europe.

It was in Vienna that disaster almost struck. Perhaps seeing that Masoud Barzani was the one most likely to take over the cause of Kurdish independence from his father, and perhaps fearing how successful he was likely to be at it, Iraqi intelligence officers attempted to assassinate him. One of his aides was wounded in the attack, but Masoud Barzani was able to survive it and continue. He made it to Tehran in 1979, in the wake of the Iranian revolution, helping to maintain relations with the new Iranian regime as Kurdish forces initially helped with the Shah's overthrow.

It was only while he was there that he received the news that his father, Mullah Mustafa Barzani, had died from the cancer he had suffered from for several years. What must it have been like for him in that moment? He had been aware of his father's illness, must have been aware that this news could have come at any moment, but at the same time, such news is always a shock when it does come.

Preparations had already been put in place, of course. Part of the reason that Masoud Barzani was travelling was that his father was too ill to do so, and obviously for several years, he had been acting on his father's behalf as an emissary, and as a leader within the KDP. Now though, there were things that needed to be done. The most important for the moment was the return of his father's body to the region, although it was impossible to return it to the Barzani areas of Kurdistan, since access to Iraq was prevented.

There was one more thing to follow. Mullah Mustafa Barzani's death had left a gap, and the KDP needed a leader. Were there other contenders for that position, besides Masoud Barzani? Who else might have been able to perform the role? Perhaps Idris Barzani could have, but somewhere in the previous few years, it seems that he had fallen more into the role of staying by his father's side why Masoud Barzani was more active in connecting with Kurdistan's allies abroad. Perhaps it was a matter that was already decided between them, with them having agreed that Masoud Barzani would be the more appropriate candidate for the leadership.

Certainly, he had many qualities that made him a good candidate. He had experience of leading both militarily and politically, because his father had pushed him to do both. He had already established relations with international leaders, because he had spent time as an emissary and negotiator on his father's behalf. His role in the establishment of the Parastin and in helping to secure Mullah Mustafa Barzani's position meant that he had the tools and the understanding to maintain unity within the KDP.

Could someone else have become the leader? There may be some question marks about the way in which Masoud Barzani became leader, with the suggestion that it happened simply because he was Mullah Mustafa Barzani's son. There are probably those to whom it seems more like the transfer of power in a monarchy than in a democracy.

Possibly, but in this case it seems that Masoud Barzani was genuinely the most qualified person for the job. It seems unlikely that anyone else could have done as good a job, that they would have had the connections or the experience. The simple fact is that Masoud Barzani had been groomed from birth to be a leader, had been taught the skills he needed for the role, and had the symbolic power of expectation behind him.

In the ninth party conference of the KDP, in 1979, the transition of power became official; Masoud Barzani was confirmed as the president of the KDP, moving from a position in which he already had influence to one in which he had formal power, from one in which people went along with him out of respect for his achievements to one in which he could now expect that the structures of the KDP would act as he required them to.

There was a noticeable difference in power that went with the position, but also a difference in responsibility, especially going into a decade that was to prove to be one of the most difficult for the people of Kurdistan, both for those he led and for those who were simply caught up in the violence.

CHAPTER FOUR

The 1980s

THE 1980S REPRESENT a key decade for Masoud Barzani. He'd been an important figure in the KDP before, but this was the first decade in which he was its leader. It was the first chance that he'd had to truly make a difference for his people, and the first time that he'd truly had control of the decision-making processes of the party. It was also the period in which he, the Barzanis, the KDP, and Kurdistan as a whole would face the most significant threats that they ever had, including threats to their very existence.

Iran-Iraq Conflict

When we are talking about Masoud Barzani's life in the 1980s, we are now talking clearly about the life of a leader whose decisions could affect the lives and well-being of thousands, if not tens of thousands, of people. As the KDP's leader, he had a key role to play in all aspects of the struggle for independence, whether it was trying to determine the correct disposition of peshmerga forces, or trying to establish the best way to get supplies to those working from the mountains. At the same time, this was a period immediately after the loss of his father in 1979, when he was trying to come to terms with this new role.

Yet in spite of his position as a leader, we must recognise that Masoud Barzani did not have absolute control over the things that happened around him. The decisions he made had to be reactions to events as much as part of a broader plan, and they could only take place within the broader context of the region.

In the 1980s, that context was largely one of violence between Iran and Iraq, in the form of the Iran-Iraq war. It began on the 22nd September 1980, when Iraqi forces moved into Iranian territories, but its roots go back much further. In the short term, the reasons included a desire to overturn the terms of the Algiers Agreement that had brought an end to conflict between the two countries in 1975, and unresolved tensions from that previous round of violence.

In the longer term, the very existence of the two countries was likely to promote conflict between them, indeed, it was designed to do so. The treaties that did so much to harm Kurdistan at the end of the First World War also set up other conflicts in the region, and that between Iran and Iraq is an obvious example. Iraq was always intended to be a counterbalance to Iran, set up to be a country of sufficient power to slow down any expansionist tendencies on its part. It was put in place to limit the resurgence of a Persian empire to fill the void left by the demise of the Ottoman one, in the typically colonialist belief that the east had no right to a great power to rival those of Europe or the US. Put like that, violence seems designed into Iraq's existence.

It certainly happened in 1980. While it had briefly seemed as though the two countries were heading for greater reconciliation in the late 1970s, with each effectively handing over assets to the other for show trials and executions, the truth was that this was never likely to be more than a brief period of truce and rearmament.

Certainly that became the case after the Iranian revolution in 1979. While Iraq made brief overtures of friendship towards the newly emerged regime in its neighbour, those were quickly rejected, with the Iranian government calling out for a similar revolution in Iraq, and setting itself at odds with Iraq's Ba'athist government. The result was a military build up, with Iraq believing that Iran would be weak so soon after the purges that had come with its change of government, and with sanctions in place that had taken away much of the regime's logistical support for things like heavy armour and air power. However, Iraq appears to have severely overestimated the extent to which the changes weakened Iran, which still had more than a thousand tanks, and whose newly promoted officers now owed their loyalty completely to the regime.

A series of small border disputes followed, the most serious of which was over the Shatt al-Arab waterway in 1980. We can see these either as a build up of flash points that eventually turned into a conflagration, or as simply a reflection of growing tensions that were always going to result in war.

When war came, it was bloody and relentless, starting with a full scale invasion by Iraq in September 1980, with strikes on Iranian airfields followed by an invasion along a four hundred mile front. The idea was clearly to take out the most dangerous part of the Iranian military (its air force) and then overwhelm what was left by forcing it to react across too broad a front for its supposedly decimated command structure to manage. Initially, the Iraqi forces were correct in this assumption, but quickly found themselves facing significant resistance, including attacks on their own bases.

There is no room here to go into the full details of the war, and most of them are simply not relevant. What is relevant is that from 1980–1988 Iran and Iraq waged a bloody ongoing conflict, with both sides often stuck on a defensive footing as their pushes against one another ran out of steam, and that they often did so through the use of proxies, encouraging potential rebel groups within the other's country to rise up in an attempt to weaken them. Kurdish separatists in Iraq with existing links to Iran were an obvious choice for such a role, especially when the KDP had played it before, in the 1970s.

In this sense then, the Iran-Iraq war forms vital context for this phase of Masoud Barzani's life. Without it, there would not have been the same encouragement to rise up that there was, nor the same opportunity to do so. At the same time, the war created brutal, genocidal responses from the Iraqi regime, first in 1983 and then in 1988. Without the Iran-Iraq war, politics in Iraq might have been very different, and certainly Masoud Barzani's role would have been.

Even the ending of the war had a crucial role to play in the things that happened in Kurdistan. As has proved to be the case so often in history, the ends of wars are more dangerous for Kurdistan than their progress. Rebellions that are ignored in wartime now have the full attention of a government, often one that has years of war to ready it to use force. That proved to be the case in 1988, just as it was in 1945 and 1975.

1983 Revolt

The 1983 revolt is often seen in terms that are not its own. It is often seen as a proxy war, existing purely for the benefit of the Iranian government who sponsored Kurdish fighters. It is sometimes seen as an act of foolishness, with commentators often wondering why the Kurds would revolt, knowing how the Iraqi government would respond. With that in mind, it is sometimes seen as no more than the spark that lit the geno-cides to come, including the Anfal.

Each of these may have some basis in truth, but they also miss the point. Yes, the Kurdish rebellion in 1983 received support from the Iranians to assist with their own objectives, but there would have been no rebellion for them to support without exist-ing Kurdish grievances. The questions about what came next, meanwhile, seem to ask that the leaders of the rebellion should have had the ability to see into the future. They are criticisms made with hindsight, and with a view of history that essentially removes the motives of the rebellion's true leaders.

As the leader of the KDP, Masoud Barzani was one of those leaders. What made him agree to be a part of something that seems, in hindsight, like the repetition of an old pattern where outside forces picked up and then abandoned the cause of Kurdish independence? Did he have any way to foresee the dangers that would come?

The hardest thing to do at this point is to put thoughts of the Anfal to one side. We must look at events with an understanding of the information that was available at the time. With the benefit of looking back, we know what came next, but Masoud Barzani had no way to know how the government would react. He knew that it had authoritarian tendencies, but so did every government of Iraq before it. He knew that it would fight back with deadly force, but again, that made it no different to any other revolt before.

We have to consider the history of the rebellions that he'd heard about or been involved with. In all of these, outside support or wider conflicts had been the only things that had allowed rebellions to happen at all. He would have seen the way that support could be withdrawn, abandoning rebellions to their fate, but he would also have seen that the fighters involved generally managed to enter exile safely, and often managed to force long term concessions from the government, simply by keeping up the sense of pressure.

That idea of pressure may also have played a role in Masoud Barzani's decision making. He may have hoped that this time the advances they made would be enough to result in permanent gains, but he may also have thought that, even if this revolt did not succeed, perhaps it would set up the next, and the one beyond that. At the very least, it would keep alive the idea of Kurdish independence. After all, Masoud Barzani had seen the failure of the 1976 rebellion less than a decade before, but must also have seen the support it gained, and may have felt that this time, with more committed Iranian support, there might be a better chance to build a level of independence that they could hold onto.

There is a downside to this idea of pressure, or momentum, as well, which is that when opportunities come along, they must be taken, or there is a danger of losing support for the idea of independence. Other voices come to the fore, trying to tell people that their lives are ok, or that they should concentrate on internal issues. The support for independence might still be there at the back of people's minds, but it is not mobilised.

We must also remember that Masoud Barzani was not the only one making decisions in 1983. He was the leader of the KDP, and thus had a key role to play in the decision to rebel, but there were others as well, and there was the general desire of its members to do so. It might even be fair to say that he could no more have held back referendum than the tide, had he wished to make the attempt.

The rebellion had to rely on guerrilla tactics from the start, because direct confrontation with the Iraqi army would have resulted in immediate failure. The mountains were an asset in this, providing terrain in which it was impossible for tanks and heavy armour to target the peshmerga directly. It meant that Kurdish forces were able to hit and run repeatedly, as they had always done in the past, striking at the edges of their forces, with minimal direct casualties.

Part of what this meant was the engagement of local populations, training some of them in the use of captured weaponry, providing them with security to guarantee their support and often seeking to persuade them of the value of their cause in the hopes of attracting more fighters to the peshmerga. This would ultimately have devastating repercussions, because it conflated the wider Kurdish population with the forces rebelling against the government, thus reinforcing the idea in the regime's minds that all Kurds were a potential threat to it. It was this thinking that would later result in the horrors of the Anfal, but even in this early phase, the Iraqi army employed brutal tactics.

The use of heavy armour and high numbers of troops were both well established within Kurdistan as tactics against peshmerga forces. The use of air power that the KDP had no way to counter was another facet that had been used for decades. One new element, however, was the use of grid-based bombing, where the Iraqi forces would target a defined area on a map indiscriminately, either from the air or using artillery, aiming for total destruction. It was a tactic that would later come to include the use of chemical weapons.

1983 Massacre

The mass murder of 1983 was a low point in Kurdistan's history, only prevented from being the worst moment by those that followed. It is a massacre that is often eclipsed by the larger genocide of the Anfal five years later, but it is no less important, as it represents one of the first coordinated attempts to wipe out a subset of the Kurds: specifically, the Barzanis.

The attempted genocide came in response to the revolt of 1983, representing the culmination of tactics by the Iraqi government that had already involved the targeting of civilian areas with heavy artillery and air strikes. The government had used a grid pattern to target areas apparently at random, in order to produce maximum terror.

The massacre was a step beyond even that.

Perhaps seeing the rebellion as an essentially Barzani one, due to the involvement of the KDP, or perhaps seeing the Barzanis as key figures in the wider pressures towards Kurdish independence, the government seems to have reasoned that eliminating all Barzani men and boys of fighting age would reduce the danger of revolts from Kurdistan. Already, it had many Kurds under its control, rounded up into camps and de facto ghettos, which they could not leave without the appropriate permissions.

The massacre, which has since been recognised as an act of genocide thanks to the consistent efforts of Masoud Barzani and others, took place on the 31st of July 1983. On that day, between 5000 and 8000 Barzani men and boys were taken from the euphemistically named 'resettlement camps', and were never seen again. We now know that the tactics employed by the Iraqi government elsewhere were to take those they wished to kill into the desert, dig pits with bulldozers, and then either machine gun or bulldoze those people to murder them. It thus seems likely that the same approach was used, although the exact spots of all the mass burials have not been found.

When the Iraqi army came to collect men to murder them, it came in large groups, with trucks ready to take them away. This explains some of why the men went with them: they simply had no choice. They undoubtedly knew that if they resisted, they would simply be killed on the spot, and that this might also cost the lives of the women and children there. Indeed, several women were killed as they tried to follow or stop their husbands from going. The men did not have weapons, and had no way to resist, but the government took them to their deaths anyway. Of course, they did not put it like that. Instead, they claimed that Saddam wanted to talk with them, to negotiate. Perhaps many of them believed it, or at least wanted to believe it. The government had held talks before, and tried to come to settlements with the Barzanis in the wake of conflicts, as in 1970. Failing that, many might have assumed that they would be resettled away from their families, or maybe forced to fight in the Iran-Iraq hostilities.

We now know that none of that happened, and that the men who were taken were murdered, systematically, and with the full knowledge of senior members of the government. Survival was largely a matter of chance, based purely on who the regime was able to seize in that moment.

Masoud Barzani would definitely have been a target if he had been in the camps, but instead he was out fighting against the government with the peshmerga, a part of the revolt that was seeking to establish independence while Iran and Iraq distracted one another with their conflict. His very engagement in the fight against the regime repressing Kurdistan served to save his life in that moment.

That does not mean that he avoided the pain of this moment, though. The people who died were Barzanis, those closest to him and his family. Twenty-seven of his family members were amongst those taken by the regime to be killed. The immediate impact of this loss must have been horrific, hearing about it and knowing that it was already too late to do anything about it. There may have been feelings of what is commonly termed survivor's guilt for him, with the constant asking by those who survived why they were the ones to do so.

Of course, the only real guilt lies with the evil government that elected to murder so many people. It was an act that fundamentally reshaped Kurdish society, taking away so many of the men of one generation at once. It left families without fathers, wives without husbands. The knock on effects of it for Kurdistan have been huge, including such things as the much more important place accorded to women compared to many of the surrounding societies. Simply, with so many of the men gone, Kurdistan's women got a chance to occupy roles they otherwise wouldn't have, and Kurdistan got used to the idea.

The effects on Masoud Barzani must also have been huge. He wasn't present, but he saw the evil that the government was capable of inflicting. He saw in that moment that it was truly a fight for survival for Kurdistan, not just a nationalist conflict for independence. Seeing a government prepared to slaughter the people he was committed to protecting must have hardened his resolve.

Moments like this, though, also seem to have had another effect on Masoud Barzani: they made him determined not to turn into the kind of person who could do something like that. They showed him how easily figures with great power could use that power in ways that harm others, and how their actions have consequences. It showed him first hand how harmful the instincts of dictators could be, giving him a reference point when he was later in a position of power as Kurdistan's president.

It is hard to treat 1983 and its effects with the seriousness that it deserves, not because of any lack of seriousness, but because of what happened next. If nothing else had happened afterwards, then we would look back today at 1983 and the genocide that it involved with horror. Instead, it has become a precursor, a prologue, to what came next, seen as only the first wave of a greater project of extermination: the Anfal.

Idris Barzani's Death

One key event happened in 1987 that reshaped both Masoud Barzani's life and the KDP as a whole: the death of his brother, Idris Barzani from a heart attack. That death came suddenly, while he was in exile with other elements of the KDP's political structure, in Iran.

Because this work has been about Masoud Barzani, it has often glossed over his brother's work, yet it is hard to over-estimate the impact that his loss would have had, especially coming less than a decade after their father's death, and immediately before what was to be the most grief filled time for all of Kurdistan.

In the preceding decades, Idris Barzani had worked as closely with their father as Masoud Barzani had. He had been a key player in the production of the KDP's political structures in exile, in the consolidation of power within Kurdistan, and in Kurdistan's relations with its allies. He had often been sent abroad to speak with the major players in other political systems to try to secure support, yet he had just as often been by their father's side when Masoud Barzani was the one sent off on such tasks. It was such an arrangement that meant that

Idris Barzani was one of those at Mullah Mustafa Barzani's side when he passed away.

These roles can only hint at everything that Masoud Barzani lost when Idris Barzani died, because of course, he lost a brother as well, and we must never lose sight of the impact of normal human emotions on leaders. We may think of them as something else, something special, even as something more akin to symbolic figures than real people, yet in their hearts, every leader has all the emotions that move all of us. The loss of a brother like that would have been as devastating for Masoud Barzani as anyone else, would have left him grieving right at the moment when Kurdistan needed him the most.

There were impacts in terms of running the KDP, too. Idris Barzani's death meant that even more of the responsibility than before landed on Masoud Barzani's shoulders. He had been leader of the party for eight years at this point, but his brother's presence had given him a sounding board of his generation he could trust, a confidante and someone he could trust to make the right decisions in his absence. Probably, his plans for running the KDP for the coming decades all had Idris Barzani at their heart, and now he had to rework those plans and expectations, trying to understand how things would work in the future.

The shock for the KDP would have been just as great. Idris Barzani was a key figure within it, and in those days when party structures were largely dependent on the individuals involved, his loss was a hole that would not easily be filled. Instantly, the KDP lost the relationships he had built up with political figures both in Kurdistan and abroad, lost his particular insight into events, and lost the small level of public recognition he had built around the world alongside his father.

It is a common game in historical circles to imagine what events might have been like if things had been different, as a way of understanding causes and their impact. If we try to imagine the way that things might have turned out without this cause or that cause, we have a tool with which to work out the relative important of different factors. Obviously, such exercises are subject to the chaotic knock on effects of many other influences, so that we can never be certain how things would have turned out, but we can at least make a guess. Two such scenarios present themselves here.

Firstly, what would it have been like if Idris Barzani had survived? Would his additional contacts abroad have been able to secure more and quicker support for Kurdistan during the Anfal and beyond? Perhaps, in a small way, yet the story of Kurdistan has always been of its allies being pleasant in person, but then not coming through for when Kurdistan finds itself in danger. Perhaps his additional presence could have added to the speed of the KDP's response, and perhaps in the later period of the civil war, he might have been able to act as a go between, but even these things seem limited in scope.

Secondly, and more seriously, what would things be like for Kurdistan if Masoud Barzani had been the one to die in 1987, and not his brother? Would it have just been a like for like swap, with events unchanged? After all, both were of a similar age, had seen similar trajectories through the party, and their share of conflicts. Both had spent time by their father's side, and had achieved senior positions within the KDP.

Yet there were differences that might have meant significant changes for the KDP. By 1987, Masoud Barzani was entrenched as its leader, and as the successor to his father. His loss at that point would have caused even greater disruption than Idris Barzani's death did. He was the public face of the KDP, which would have meant their alliances taking a hit. Considering later events, we must suggest that it was Masoud Barzani's personality as much as his name or training that allowed him to succeed as president, and to push Kurdistan towards the referendum that will, for better or worse, forever be associated with his presidency. While Idris Barzani was an important figure in the KDP in the 1970s and 80s, it seems unreasonable to suggest that things would have turned out the same had his and his brother's positions been reversed in 1987.

That is not to say that his loss had no impact. It was a devastating moment both for Masoud Barzani and the KDP. However, the impact of that loss is hard to see at this remove in history, because any disruption it caused was dwarfed by the disruption and death that followed. Idris Barzani's death was a tragedy in 1987, but just a year later, a far greater tragedy was to follow: the Anfal.

CHAPTER FIVE

The Anfal

THE ANFAL HAS been recognised internationally as a genocide, but only after more than two decades of work to persuade the world that it met the definition. This reluctance largely came from an unwillingness on the part of some members of the international community to admit that they should have been involved in stopping it, as is required in the case of genocides under the UN's rules. Were it not for this deliberate avoidance, it would be hard to see how it could ever have been classified as anything else. It was a programme of mass murder that resulted in the deaths of more than a hundred thousand people, along with the destruction of more than 4000 of Kurdistan's villages, as part of a process of displacement that resulted in more than a million people fleeing the country.

The core of the Anfal took place in 1988, with the use of both conventional and chemical weapons against civilian targets. Often, the process involved the bombardment of set-tlements by the army, followed by the use of troops to mop up survivors. However, it took place in a number of distinct phases, of which the 1983 massacre might be considered the first. Certainly, it was a precursor to what followed, perhaps even a test run, aimed at establishing protocols that would allow Baghdad to kill as many of Kurdistan's inhabitants as possible.

Officially though, the Anfal is usually divided into a series of phases in 1988. Why then? Largely because the Iran-Iraq war that had officially been going since 1980 was meandering down towards a cessation, brokered by international partners. Such moments have always been dangerous for Kurdish rebellions, and for the one that started in 1983, this was to prove devastating. It wasn't just the potential withdrawal of support from Iran that was to prove deadly, but the freedom of the Iraqi army to act within Kurdistan without the fear of Iranian reprisals, or the need to worry about conflict with anyone but the peshmerga.

The Anfal was not one thing, but a series of attacks, each using different tactics. It may be useful to go through those phases to understand the enormity of that situation. The first phase in 1988 involved multiple attacks on villages, leading up to the attack on Halabja, using poison gas. The second phase, from March to April 1988, targeted areas south-west of Sulaymaniyah, using poison gas attacks to force people to flee villages, and then using conventional forces to try to capture and kill those who fled, in an escalation of the tactics of the first phase. The third phase took place later in April, targeting settlements east of Sulaymaniyah. In this phase, the tactics of the first two phases were repeated, combined with the use of disinformation to lure Kurdish peshmerga and civilians into areas where they could be killed.

The fourth phase, in May, saw the attacks move towards Erbil and Kirkuk, targeting the areas that formed the boundary between them. The next three phases targeted valleys of Rawandiz and Shaqlawa, in a series of attacks that seemed more like conventional military attacks, and that initially involved deals with dissident elements of the Iraqi forces to allow some civilians to escape.

During the eighth and final phase, from August to September, KDP held areas were specifically targeted, again featuring the use of chemical attacks. The Iraqi army also deliberately sought to cut off the route to the Turkish border, giving those people who had to run nowhere to go. Again, the army sought to capture those who were in the process of escaping, killing the men while forcing the women and children into concentration camps similar to those that had already been tested against the Barzanis in the early 1980s.

Adult men seem to have been particularly heavily targeted throughout the phases of the Anfal, although the indiscriminate nature of many of the attacks and the horrendous conditions of imprisonment mean that thousands of women died too. Perhaps this division was in part because one of the early aims of the Anfal was to attempt to eliminate all potential men who might be able to take part in future rounds of fighting against the regime. It was, as many genocides are, an extension of the desire to eliminate an opposing force that could not clearly be distinguished from the general population. In such circumstances, the response of some regimes is to assume that only the total elimination of all men who might fight back is sufficient.

The result was huge disruption to Kurdistan's population. Estimates of the death count from the Anfal vary wildly, with a few as low as 50,000, but more official Kurdish sources placing the number closer to 182,000. This figure is before we take into account the million or so people who were forced to flee the country, internally displaced, or imprisoned. Such displacement is recognised in international law as being just as much of a war crime as mass murder, and with good reason: it devastates families and countries just as efficiently, and is just as clearly a matter of ethnic cleansing.

In some ways, an even more telling figure is that, in the areas the Anfal targeted, more than 90% of all villages were destroyed. In was a practice aimed at the urbanisation of the population in ways that might be more controllable by the regime, and one that fundamentally changed Kurdistan as a region. It took it from being a region of small communities dotted around mountains and valleys, to being one where the majority of the population are city dwellers. It devastated Kurdistan's farming infrastructure, making it reliant for a long time on imports supported by black market oil sales. It also meant significant cultural damage for Kurdistan, eliminating many of the environments in which its more traditional cultures had thrived, so that only government action was able to preserve them.

At the same time, the Anfal involved a process of Arabization that involved luring people from the south to repopulate areas where the local population had been driven out or murdered.

This aspect of the Anfal has had some of its most pernicious long term effects, creating conflicts that persist to this day over areas that were traditionally Kurdish, but now have well established Arab populations that are often into their second generation and now view those regions as home.

It is hard to summarise the evil of the Anfal in such a short space, but this is not a book about the Anfal; it is about Masoud Barzani. The Anfal was one of the greatest challenges he faced in his life, so how did he respond to it? What did he do in the face of such an existential threat to his people?

Masoud Barzani's Role

As with many periods of his life, it is hard to pin down exactly where Masoud Barzani was at what time during this phase. Now though, it has nothing to do with the shadow of his father obscuring his presence, and everything to do with a time when it is hard to know where anyone in Kurdistan was exactly. The Anfal was a time of huge disruption, where there was hardly the time to keep records of who was where, unless someone had the misfortune to be captured by the regime, which Masoud Barzani was not. We are able to trace him indirectly, however, since he was the head of the KDP's peshmerga forces, and was engaged in leading the efforts to fight back against the regime, both during the 1983 revolt and afterwards.

We know that he was the force behind much of the initial success of the 1983 revolt. He was the one who had made a deal with Iran for assistance, briefly helping it to fight domestic uprisings in Iran in return for help fighting Iraq. Perhaps he should have seen that a country so interested in putting down its own rebels would have no real interest in helping those of its neighbour for their own sake; it was only interested in the disruption that KDP forces could cause to Iraq.

Probably, he did see this. After all, he was aware of how quickly others had abandoned the KDP in the past. My suspicion is that Masoud Barzani took a calculated risk, knowing that Iranian interest in the KDP would only last as long as its conflict with Iraq, but also hoping that its need for a buffer zone in the wake of any conflict might pave the way towards a more independent Kurdistan.

We also know that for much of the 1980s, he was actively engaged in the fight against the Iraqi regime. He was instrumental in coordinating most of the efforts of the peshmerga during the initial rebellion, and their successes in that phase was at least partly due to the tactics that he had learned and the structures that he had helped to put int place to coordinate the efforts of the KDP. Without the organisations that he had helped to found during the years of exile, would that continued rebellion have been possible?

In 1983, and during the Anfal, Masoud Barzani was saved largely because of his engagement in the fighting. The attacks targeted Kurdish villages, but he and the other peshmerga were in the mountains, moving back and forth between Iraq and Iran. In that sense, the conflict that should have placed him in greater danger actually helped to prevent his capture or death.

It must have weighed on him that civilians were being targeted in the wake of a rebellion that he had helped to propel. Even though true responsibility lay only with the Baghdad regime, he must have worried that his continuing rebellion contributed to the excuse for that violence. Yet what else could he have done? Stood by and allowed Baghdad to erase his people, destroy his culture, wipe out the legitimate claim they had on the land they had lived on for centuries?

Certainly, once the violence against the people of Kurdistan had begun, the only thing for him to do was to keep fighting, trying to protect those people from the violence that fell on them.

We know in this period that the peshmerga did try to move from place to place, avoiding the most obvious attacks by the army, yet at the same time, they often had to put themselves in harm's way in order to defend the civilian populations of the region. They did so at Masoud Barzani's command, often risking their lives in the hope that they would be able to buy ordinary people time to flee, or space to escape through.

What must it have been like, trying to think of tactics that might work in a situation that was essentially hopeless? We know that Masoud Barzani had been trained thoroughly int he principles of guerrilla warfare, which were largely about being able to take on such odds and hurt the enemy until they withdrew, yet how, in a situation where the Baghdad regime was inflicting such terrible suffering on the people of the region, was it possible to do anything useful? What *could* they do?

One thing we know they were able to do was to protect civilians as they sought to escape. Particularly later on, when the Gulf War made it possible to retake camps, Masoud Barzani was involved in the establishment of safe routes by which civilians could escape to Iran, yet even during the Anfal, he sought to provide ways for them to flee the onslaught of the violence. His troops ran convoys to attempt escape, and led people on foot from the more remote villages. They defended people from the Iraqi army where they could, even though the air power and chemical weapons at the Baghdad regime's disposal meant that there were far too many situations in which they knew that they could *not* help.

We must remember before levelling any criticism for that inability that it was simply a consequence of the difference in power of the forces involved. Masoud Barzani, and those around him, had to struggle just to survive alongside the rest of Kurdistan when faced with such an existential threat. It is fair to say that without the presence of the peshmerga under his command, the destruction during the Anfal might have been even more total. As it was, they were able to save at least some people.

Mostly though, the only action available to them during the genocide was to wait. They had to find hidden positions within the mountains, had to slip over the border, had to keep moving. They had to trust that eventually the storm of destruction would pass, and the situation would change. It eventually did, with the advent of the First Gulf War, and the result was a chance to finally free Kurdistan from some of the horrors that it had suffered. It was a chance that Masoud Barzani would take gratefully.

Masoud Barzani and the Legacy of the Anfal

One of the key roles that Masoud Barzani has played in the wake of the Anfal has been in not allowing its legacy to be forgotten.

He has fought for its recognition as a genocide, and crucially has sought the recognition of the massacre of 1983 as such as well. With an atrocity that was so personal to him, this is hardly surprising; he lost friends and family members, along with so many others. At the same time, his role in talking to the international community about this has been one that many others would not have taken on.

This is especially true when there has often been pressure from outside to ignore the Anfal, or to treat it as a purely Kurdish matter. That is an approach that seeks to minimise it, or to ignore its impact on subsequent events. Masoud Barzani seems to have understood that permitting such things to be forgotten increases the chances of them happening again.

Keeping memories of the genocide alive has proved particularly important when it comes to explaining Kurdistan's actions and allowing the world to understand its relationships with its neighbours. It is only the memory of that genocide that makes it possible for Kurdistan to explain why relations with the surrounding countries are important, and why independence remains important for Kurdistan's inhabitants. It is not enough to make a claim based on ancient separation from other ethnic groups in the wider region, or even to stress the consistency with which the Kurds have sought to assert their independence from the countries that have trapped them within them. It *might* be enough to make the case that they cannot be safe in any other way; that only by being separate from the governments that might harm them can they be sure that those governments will not repeat the outcomes of the Anfal.

He was a key force in making sure that 16th March was commemorated as Halabja Memorial Day, with the result that it is commemorated annually in Kurdistan, keeping alive the memories of the genocide that contained the attack on that city. He has also, as president and in his new role as a respected public figure, played a key part in those commemorations, serving as a living connection to the events of that past.

In some ways, we can also suggest that the memory of the Anfal has been instrumental in Masoud Barzani's political programme, and not just in the furtherance of the cause of independence. Yes, of course, memories of the genocides have been key factors in pushing Kurdistan towards independence. They have been crucial in sowing distrust between Baghdad and Kurdistan, ensuring that a solution that keeps Kurdistan under the control of Baghdad remains unacceptable to much of its people.

But it was the destruction wrought by it that meant that he later had to do so much in terms of reconstruction as president. He and the KDP worked hard, first in their own areas, and then in Kurdistan as a whole, to undo some of the damage that was wrought by the Anfal. In seeking to undo some of the physical scars of the conflict, Masoud Barzani gained much of the impetus for his domestic reforms.

It also shaped him as a president. Where many presidents of the region have been quick to dismiss human rights abuses, and to attack their enemies, Masoud Barzani and the KDP have slowly pushed for greater protections of rights within Kurdistan, and have sought to avoid becoming that kind of ruling regime. The president has done so based on the memory of the violence inflicted on him and his people.

Those have been long term legacies, though. What of the position of Masoud Barzani and those around him at the end of the 1980s? Because of the flight from Kurdistan, he was initially no longer within the region, although as part of the rear-guard to protect that exodus, he was one of the last to leave. He saw with his own eyes some of the worst of what happened, and found himself in a position not dissimilar to that of his father in earlier times: as the leader of a group that was dispossessed, unable to return. For a brief period, it must have seemed that a return to Iraq had become an impossibility, perhaps decades away, if it was to come at all.

Certainly, there was no inkling of help from outside Kurdistan in that period. No one had shown any interest in intervening in the genocide. Indeed, until quite late in it, there was no sign of it making the news around the world. That was something that taught Masoud Barzani the value of international relations, but also of maintaining a media profile. That was a lesson for later, though. In 1989, things must have seemed too bleak for that.

Indeed, that year could well be seen as one of the lowest points of Masoud Barzani's life. He had seen his people slaughtered on a vast scale, had seen them lose their homes and seen those homes destroyed. He had commanded the peshmerga who had fought to protect them as they had escaped, but that only meant that his people ended up in refuge holding camps in Iran, at the mercy of Iranian authorities who had already abandoned them to their fate in the wake of the second Iran-Iraq war. There was no obvious way to return, and no sign that the international community was prepared to do anything about the situation. As far as anyone could see, Saddam Hussein would continue in his place as ruler of Iraq, while hundreds of thousands of Kurds would continue to be displaced, having to build new lives beyond Iraqi Kurdistan's borders.

Then, in a rush, everything changed. It did so, not because of any concern for Kurdistan's situation, or even anything that Masoud Barzani did. It did so because, improbably, war broke out again in Iraq.

CHAPTER SIX

1991

The Gulf War of 2 August 1990–28 February 1991 was a major event in the history of Kurdistan, and provided Masoud Barzani with a major opportunity to act on the region's behalf.

The Gulf War's official cause was the Iraqi invasion of Kuwait, which had significant oil supplies. It seems clear that this had little to do with Kurdistan, or everything that it had suffered to that point. Indeed, Western powers actively avoided recognising the Anfal as a genocide, specifically so that they would not be called upon to intervene before this point.

Yet the invasion of Iraq by an American led coalition had a number of beneficial effects for Kurdistan. The first was to draw away Iraqi forces from the region, forcing them to try to deal with an attack by a superior military power. Another was an opportunity to draw international attention to an area that had largely been out of the public eye in the preceding decade.

The most crucial effect came in 1991, as domestic pressures in the US started to bring the conflict to an end. Knowing that it would be necessary to withdraw ground troops, the Americans did two things that changed the course of events for Kurdistan: first, the coalition imposed a ban on fixed wing aircraft flying over the country from the 3rd of March on. Second, George Bush called on Iraq to revolt, calling for the overthrow of Saddam Hussein. This was no ordinary revolt, though, limited to Kurdistan, because groups in the South of Iraq, particularly the Marsh Arabs, chose that moment to revolt as well.

Masoud Barzani was at the heart of Kurdistan's revolt, helping to coordinate it and serving as one of the key leaders of the disparate Kurdish forces. Under his leadership, progress was swift, and one of the first things that the revolt did was to free the many people who were still trapped in so called 'resettlement camps', waiting for the government to murder them. It must have been a particularly proud moment for him, after so many years of being unable to stop mass murder, to be able to finally free those people.

The revolt didn't stop there. For a few brief weeks it spread like wildfire, with Kurdish forces spreading out to take ground to the limits of Kurdistan and almost all of the major cities of Iraq falling to other forces. Only Baghdad remained un-captured by the forces of the would be revolution.

The actual details of the revolt vary by where it was happening. The Kurdish revolt was, strictly speaking, the second phase of the uprising, coming after the one in the south, from the 5th of March on. It took a little longer because the revolt was more organised, with Kurdistan's political factions, including the KDP under Masoud Barzani, working to coordinate the actions of the peshmerga involved. Even Kurdish elements of the Iraqi army, often press ganged into service against their will, defected en masse to join the revolt. By the 20th of March, they had control of every major city in Kurdistan, with 50000 or more troops defecting to their side. It was during this uprising, and the taking of multiple Iraqi Security Service bases, that the peshmerga were able to capture literally tons of documents relating to the regime's actions during the Anfal, providing an evidence base that would later allow for it to be labelled as the genocide it was.

What must Masoud Barzani have felt during this uprising? As widespread as it was, it must have felt closer to the possibility of a free Kurdistan than at almost any point in his life. It must have seemed that Kurdistan was going to be in a position to take its independence. At the same time, though, he had lived through the revolution of 1958, so he must have known the ways that even a successful revolution could eventually turn against Kurdistan.

This revolt was not successful, though. It came so close to succeeding, so why, ultimately, did the revolt fail? Was there anything that Masoud Barzani could have done to prevent that failure?

The revolt's great weakness was also its greatest strength: it encompassed numerous disparate groups. Even in Kurdistan, there were at least two political groups working together as part of the revolt, while across Iraq, there were dozens of organisations, leaning left and right politically, representing different ethnic groups, or seeking regional autonomy for specific areas.

In the short term, this was an amazing benefit for the uprising. It meant that the Iraqi army found itself faced with attacks on multiple fronts, often without warning and in areas where it could not bring enough troops to bear. Faced with it, all the Iraqi army could do was continue to withdraw towards Baghdad. The wide spread of the revolt meant that almost instantly, there was no coherent space beyond Baghdad that the Iraqi government could call its own.

The downside to it was that it made long term coordination of what came next almost impossible. The initial wave of revolts had forced the Iraqi army back to Baghdad, but had not destroyed it. Instead, what was left of its armoured divisions and soldiers were now concentrated in the one area where no uprising had occurred, able to strike as a group against those who had risen up.

At this phase, there is a case for saying that Masoud Barzani could have brought troops south. There were some calls in Kurdistan for that to happen, but ultimately, Kurdish forces elected not to act except to secure the limits of Kurdistan.

Why was this the case? What would motive Masoud Barzani, in particular, not to take forces south to finish off the enemy who had slaughtered the Kurdish people? Part of the answer to that may be the speed with which events happened. Organising a revolt in areas one knows well is different from organising the march of an army to take new territory.

Another part of it was probably the sense that Kurdish forces would not be welcomed. I have written about the fragmented nature of the forces on the ground in the south, but we must also take into account the ethnically fragmented nature of Iraq in general. It is likely that an army of peshmerga marching south would have been seen as invaders, not allies.

Added to this, there may have been a sense of the need for Kurdistan to look after itself, founded on a sense of being ethnically separate, on the need to continue working towards the goal of independence, and perhaps on a sense that the south had done nothing to help Kurdistan in its hour of need.

Masoud Barzani would also have been aware of the potentially fleeting nature of revolts, since Kurdistan was still recovering from the aftereffects of its last attempt. As someone with military experience, he may have been better placed than most to understand that it was only a matter of time before the government counter attacked, with devastating results. He probably reasoned that, even if the revolt did succeed, a new Iraqi government would be no more likely to allow an independent Kurdistan than the existing one, and that the best option was to try to fortify Kurdistan now to make it free from outside influence.

He may even have made the mistake that so many people seem to have made, and assumed that the US invitation to revolt carried with it an implicit promise of support if it went well. There were even some calls internationally and within the US for the coalition to briefly come back and finish what it had started. Yet this was never going to happen when the US Congress had already voted against further involvement. The US call for revolt represented a last desperate attempt to get others to do what it couldn't, not a suggestion that it would be back.

Even if he had taken forces south to support the uprising there though, there is no guarantee that it would have helped. If the Kurdish peshmerga had been able to take on Saddam's forces in open battle, after all, Kurdistan would have been free many years before. It was only with the aid of the mountains that they knew that they could win, and travelling south would have deprived them of that advantage. Open ground could, and did, provide opportunities for the government's tanks to operate, while Baghdad would have been territory where the government's forces had the advantage of familiarity.

Combined with fears of being unwelcome and the sense of Kurdistan's separateness, is it really any wonder that Masoud Barzani was not willing to risk his forces? He had to hold back, both to attempt to secure the territory that his forces already held, and because of the potential risks of over extension.

In the end though, the inability of the southern rebellion to finish the Baghdad regime proved disastrous for Kurdistan, and for Iraq. The regime set about securing its base in Baghdad with ruthless efficiency, and then sent its tanks and helicopters in attacks on the Marsh Arabs of the south, winning back territory while adding to its already long list of atrocities. Helicopters were excluded from the no fly zone over the country, because they were deemed to be essential means of transport in a landscape where many river crossings had already been destroyed int he course of the Gulf War.

The combination of helicopters and tanks gave the government's forces a decisive technological advantage over the rebels standing against them. Helicopters in particular provided rapid movement along with the ability to strafe or bomb lightly armoured targets. It was a moment where the approach to warfare was changing, and the perceptions of decision makers had failed to keep up.

The result was a mass exodus from Iraq, and from Kurdistan in particular. The people freed from Saddam's camps had to flee ahead of the potential for a renewed Anfal, but there was only so fast that they could move, and there were only so many potential escape routes open to them. The border to Turkey, for example, was closed to them, with soldiers guarding against the possibility of them crossing. Some made it anyway, getting across before the Turkish government could react, but more found themselves stranded in Kurdistan, and even more had to head for Iran instead.

Someone had to slow the advancing army though, preventing it from catching up to the refugees, or even pouring over the border into Iran after them. This was where Masoud Barzani played a crucial role. This was not marching south into a country from which Kurdistan believed itself to be separate, nor did it involve committing peshmerga on terrain that they were not familiar with. Instead, this was a fight to protect their homeland, and their people. It was one that Masoud Barzani had been preparing for all his life.

He and the KDP's peshmerga, coordinating with peshmerga across Kurdistan, managed to hold back the advance of the Iraqi army in a way that insurgencies elsewhere in Iraq had not. With the no fly zone stopping the heaviest of Iraq's air support, and Kurdistan's terrain limiting the effectiveness of their armour. Using tactics perfected in the rebellions of the preceding twenty years, they were able to do more than simply fight and cover the refugees' escape: they were able to fight the Iraqi army to a standstill.

The result was that the Iraqi government was forced to concede the futility of its position, if only in part. It agreed to grant three provinces it had formerly claimed autonomous status, not out of any act of generosity, but because it suspected that it was better than the full independence, or renewed western military intervention, that might result if it pressed the issue.

Masoud Barzani was involved in the agreement to produce that autonomous region, making him one of the founders of Kurdistan as we know it today. He was brought into the initial discussions regarding the shape that the ensuing Kurdistan should take, and helped to bring about the transition from a rebellion to a self governing region. This was a crucial moment, as it is for any emerging country, because the structures and norms produced in a moment such as this can affect the shape of a region or country for generations to come.

The elections that followed, in 1992, were the first free and fair ones to be held in Kurdistan. They involved elections to the newly formed National Assembly, with 105 seats, of which five per cent were reserved for members of the Assyrian community. The results of the elections split more or less geographically between the PUK and Masoud Barzani's KDP.

What must it have been like for Masoud Barzani in that moment? He had just experienced some of the most intense fighting of his life, after a period of seeing some of the worst atrocities against the Kurds in history. Now, he was seeing the thing that he had worked towards for so long. He was going to be a part of the government of an essentially autonomous region, free from the interference of the government that had tried to hold onto it for so long. It must have been a moment of pure joy, but also a surprisingly worrying moment, too.

Why worrying? Put simply, there is a moment for every successful uprising when it must make the transition from the needs of that uprising to the needs of a stable and fair government. These are not always, or even often, the same thing. Fighting against a larger and more powerful foe requires relatively personal governance rather than systems that can be targeted. It needs movements composed of multiple parts, but also a strong sense of who is making the decisions, where countries require the space for all views to be represented and discussed. It requires a willingness to take what is needed for the cause, and to act ruthlessly against one's enemies, while governance requires the understanding that they are not enemies, but dissenting political voices.

Above all, the transition from war fighting to governance is a shift from a personal approach to a rules based one, from something held together by personality and the strength of the cause to something held together by agreed norms and a willingness to stick to the rules of the political system even when it is going against you.

Masoud Barzani showed his willingness to make that transition in the days after Kurdistan was granted autonomous status, helping to build its political structures and to write a constitution designed to work for all of those within Kurdistan, whatever their background. He showed a commitment to its political system, and to becoming a politician.

In this, he represents a step change from his father. Mullah Mustafa Barzani was the resistance leader that Kurdistan needed, but Masoud Barzani managed to both be that for much of his life and then make the change to being a political figure who had to accept a very different way for the world to work.

Things were very different in the days that followed. Reports from shortly after the withdrawal of Saddam's troops from Kurdistan state how quickly Kurdistan managed to achieve normality and order, with trust quickly rising in the police and security forces once they were no longer staffed by Baghdad loyalists. The south actively called its officials back to Baghdad, and since only the Arab officials obeyed that call, it left a cadre of Kurdish civil servants, police officers and more who were able to help with the newly autonomous region.

There were obvious challenges in this period. The after-effects of the ejected regime were still there. The deaths of so many men in such a short space of time left whole areas, such as Qushtapa, where the demographics were radically changed, while at the same time, the infrastructure of Kurdistan had been drastically damaged. Hundreds of villages were gone, while in the areas that had been built as urban prison camps, the roads, sewage systems and other amenities were missing.

At the same time, Kurdistan was cut off from potential sources of income and support. Payments from the south to officials stopped, while the south imposed an embargo on goods crossing the border into Kurdistan. This was in addition to a general embargo imposed on the whole of Iraq by the international community. Because that community refused (and refuses) to recognise Kurdistan as an independent nation, it was caught up in the same blockade designed to put pressure on Saddam's regime in the south. This meant significant hardships for Kurdistan, and significant challenges for Masoud Barzani and the KDP.

Part of the reward for that was the chance to share power. In those first elections, the KDP and the PUK received by far the largest shares of the votes, and agreed to work together within the newly formed assembly that was to govern the country. The vote was largely split along geographical lines, with the KDP receiving more votes in areas such as Erbil and Dohuk and the PUK gaining the most in Sulaymaniyah. Even today, there is a strong sense of a geographical division to Kurdish politics, as people feel a sense of connection to parties in particular areas, or see them as having played a key role in bringing freedom to those areas.

This is another key element of post uprising politics. In general, when a government is successfully overthrown in an area, or when a country or region is freed from outside influence after a struggle, there is often a sense of gratitude towards the political figures seen as having achieved it. A notable example of this is the long term electoral success of the ANC in South Africa, which continues to receive the largest share of the vote in elections decades after the overthrow of Apartheid there. At least partly, that is down to a sense that the party has already done a great deal for the people there because of its role in bringing down that system, and so there are (now mostly older) voters who will always vote for it.

In Kurdistan, the phenomenon seems to have manifested in the success of the KDP and PUK (even until today). In 1991, neither could sweep the board, but that was to be expected in a political system based on proportionality, and where multiple legitimate options existed. So long as they worked together, it seemed that they would be able to govern for the foreseeable future, and probably take Kurdistan closer and closer towards full independence.

Yet that was not what happened. Instead, after only a couple of years of government, Kurdistan found itself plunged into violence once again, this time at the hands of its own people. It was a conflict that would see Kurdistan pulled back closer to Iraq, and that would dry up international support towards it for years to come. How did it get there, and what can we say about Masoud Barzani's contentious role in the finish of the war? It is a difficult subject, but it is one that we must address if we are to fully understand his role within Kurdistan.

CHAPTER SEVEN

The Civil War

The civil war represents one of the darkest chapters of Kurdistan's history. It is harder for Kurds to discuss, in many ways, than even the Anfal, because at least that was an act of violence against all of them. The civil war, instead, involved Kurds fighting against Kurds, often with former friends and occasionally family members pitted against one another.

The brief version of its causes is usually summarised as it being a conflict for control of black market oil supplies out of Kurdistan. The truth of the causes, however, is far more complicated, and intimately involves Masoud Barzani, along with his family. It is a difficult period to write about, and does not always show Masoud Barzani in the best light, but it is important to explore it if we are to understand the things that have driven the former president throughout his time as a leader.

The causes are both as simple as commonly believed, and vastly more complicated, all at the same time. Yes, conflict over the control of black market oil formed the flash point between the KDP and PUK, but it is vital to understand the context in which this conflict came into being. We must understand that, at the end of 1991, Kurdistan was effectively cut off. The no fly zone applied to *any* fixed wing aircraft entering the airspace there, and while this protected Kurdistan, it also cut it off from the world. It limited access to the region, and this was compounded by both a blockade from the south and by largely closed borders from Kurdistan's neighbours.

In this climate, there was little aid to be found for Kurdistan. The refugees in camps beyond Kurdistan's borders received some degree of international aid, but the people within the region also had needs. They required access to food, to medicine, and more. All of those things required money, and the ability to trade across borders. Kurdistan's infrastructure had been devastated by the Anfal, and by the conflict to break free of Baghdad's control.

Regions that break free from the control of a larger country can face a number of circumstances, from relatively good ongoing relations (as in the case of Sweden and Norway, for example), to a distant relationship without significant physical damage. Kurdistan's case was worse. It was a region whose people had been displaced, whose cities had been ruined, and whose economy had been utterly destroyed. Even its agriculture was hugely damaged, because the villages that had been its backbone had been systematically attacked previously, and the people who had worked the land were gone.

Everything had to be bought into the country in those first few years; food, medicine, everything. To get the money to buy that, the groups who ruled Kurdistan had only one real resource to exploit, the same one they had exploited to fund their military operations: its oil. Yet there was a problem even with that, because oil from Iraq was under embargo, and Kurdistan was still considered a part of the country, even if it was autonomous in every respect. To gain the money to help people, oil had to be sold illicitly, smuggled out of the region to raise funds.

It was something that placed both of the main parties in a difficult position. The government as a whole could not act to sell oil, because that was forbidden under international law, yet its sale required relatively powerful groups to organise, such as them. The PUK and KDP's strong regional connections also played a role, because each felt that it had to sell oil to provide for the regions under their control. They started to do so, each finding its own paths through the mountains to sell to outside groups. It was a trade that was tolerated, even welcomed, by the surrounding countries, so that the flow of oil would keep coming in the wake of a war that seemed to have stopped it.

The conflicts over the oil began because there were only so many places that oil could be found within Kurdistan, and because each group needed control of those resources to provide for its people. It is here that we must acknowledge a second cause of the conflict: the sense that the group that could provide the most to a given region would receive political support from it, and thus have more control over the region as a whole.

This mattered because of the differing visions of Kurdistan that the different political parties in the region had. Where once the PUK and KDP had been strongly linked, now, they saw themselves in diametrically opposed terms, and neither was prepared to allow the other total control over Kurdistan. The oil was both a tool within this conflict and a marker for it.

Could the civil war have been avoided? It is always dangerous to speculate about alternative possibilities in history, because we do not know what additional factors might have come into play. We *can* say that for it to have been avoided would have required the KDP, PUK and others to agree over the disposition of Kurdistan's resources, and over the governance of the country. In the context of their history, that was always unlikely, since they had been reluctant partners at best in the years before. Yet it is possible that, with the right diplomacy and trust, maybe the tensions could have been prevented from escalating into actual violence.

It is here that Masoud Barzani was largely trapped by his past, by the allies and enemies he had already made in his life. He was not a neutral figure, who could appear to be reaching out impartially. Instead, when he acted for the good of the regions under KDP control, it must have seemed to his political opponents that he was acting to seize greater control. In this, the transition from conflict to peace also played a part, because every side was stuck in patterns of behaviour that were appropriate for the warfare that had been before, but were not yet suited to the peaceful region Kurdistan would eventually become.

These patterns included a suspicion of the motives of others, a need to act decisively rather than collaboratively, an understanding of violence as the most direct way to achieve their aims, and longstanding conflicts with one another that could not simply be set aside. Each assumed that the other side was seeking total control over the region, because the last decades had seen dictatorial control be the norm under Iraq, and because they had already had a number of small scale conflicts.

The progress of the civil war was sporadic, consisting of numerous small scale attacks by both sides. It is hard to state what that violence was truly like. The first wave of clashes may have killed more than 300 people, with another 2000 dying over the course of 1994. In the context of the conflicts that had gone before, these were relatively small numbers, but each death hurt many times more than it otherwise would have, because it was a matter of Kurds killing Kurds.

The tactics that all sides in the conflict had learned to employ meant that the civil war was never going to be a matter of pitched battles and the rapid taking of territory. The peshmerga on all sides were skilled in hit and run tactics, in rapid strikes, and in the elimination of small groups of targets. It became a war of fear, where no one knew if they were safe, and there were risks every time even ordinary people stepped outside, because they didn't know if they had been labelled as a supporter of the wrong group, or if they would be caught up in the crossfire in a battle that had nothing to do with them.

The war quickly divided the whole region into sides, with control over individual cities contested. Then, as today, Erbil was more of a KDP city, while Sulaymaniyah was in PUK control, but it was not as clear cut as that. Within each city, the other's forces sought opportunities to create disruption, while in areas where oil production provided potential resources with which to win the war, the conflict was more intense. The result was violence, death, and the disruption of normal life. Where the initial move towards autonomy had aimed to create functioning structures and new infrastructure, the civil war tore Kurdistan apart.

Initially, Kurdistan's parliament continued to meet, with America sending envoys to try to negotiate a truce, but also trying to redirect the violence towards Kurdistan's common enemy, Saddam, in an attempt to kill him in 1995. That attempt failed, but it did at least result in the capture of some Iraqi army elements, demonstrating Kurdistan's ability to protect itself. It also meant that forces that would otherwise have been devoted to the internal conflict were busy focusing on the greater enemy. There were suggestions from some of the Americans involved that there might be US support in the assault, but after 1991, it was impossible to procure.

It did at least result in a brief truce between the main sides of the conflict, with them settling into the cities where they had the greatest control. The problem was that none of the issues that had sparked the conflict had been resolved, they had just been pushed down under the surface.

It meant that a second phase of the war built, and continued, with attacks taking place again and again, followed by periods in which it seemed that there was relative peace. Part of the problem in this phase, and indeed part of the problem for Kurdistan in all its conflicts, is that the forces involved were ones better suited to sudden attacks than to taking and holding territory against the power of conventional forces. The sides could strike at one another, but it didn't make any difference to their entrenched positions in their traditional cities.

While there was a ceasefire in place, the situation in general had worsened to the point where Kurdistan's parliament could no longer meet, the country too fractured for there to be any realistic chance of its decisions being followed.

The situation might have stayed like that, caught in an uneasy, not quite peace where the battles had run out of momentum and neither side felt as though it could achieve final victory. What prompted a shift was the interference of forces from beyond Kurdistan, who saw opportunities for profit, or to strike at their enemies through intermediaries. As with so many other times in Kurdistan's history, a proxy war ended up hurting the Kurds far more than any of those who were seeking to use them to fight one another.

The starting point was the embargo on oil exports from Iraq. The sides in the conflict already had some control over smuggling routes, but when the Iraqi government demanded that the KDP assist with the illegal export of oil through Kurdistan to get it out of Iraq, the stakes rose considerably. Masoud Barzani and the KDP, it could be argued, acted in the only way that was available to them, because allowing those oil exports was a move that had the potential to both normalise relations with Iraq and that could provide KDP controlled areas with money to start to rebuild, or to buy in essential supplies. By taxing oil exports through the route they provided, the KDP was able to generate consistent revenue, which then meant that they were able to provide essential public services to the population of their areas, in a way that was made much more difficult by the effects of the surrounding embargoes.

The *problem* with this approach was that it broke the symmetry that had existed between the KDP and PUK. Where before, both sides were balanced enough that it seemed obvious that they would hang onto their existing territories, now, it must have seemed to the PUK that the KDP was gaining an advantage. On a larger scale, the same sort of question marks must have been arising between Iraq and Iran. Iran had been certain that Kurdistan would provide a useful buffer between it and its belligerent neighbour, and had also been certain that the embargo on oil would limit Iraq's capacity to strike at it. Now, with Iraq receiving money again, it was in a position where it might be able to rearm and become a threat once more.

Just as Masoud Barzani's KDP had made connections with the Iraqi government, Jalal Talabani's PUK started to forge alliances with Iran. An initial round of peace making meant that the two sides were prepared to split the profits from the arrangement, but there was insufficient oversight to compel them to stick to the deal, and in any case, it was clear to each that the other wished a bigger share of control when it came to the region. In some ways, that was even inevitable, because each needed both control and finances in order to adequately support the people of their region.

Dissatisfied with the way the deal was going, the initial incursion that broke the deadlock was from the Iranian side, invited in by the PUK. Iranian troops came over the border, and it became clear to Masoud Barzani that if things stayed as they were, then the KDP faced being wiped out, not only as a political force, but perhaps literally.

It is here that we must come to one of the most difficult decisions that Masoud Barzani has made in his career as a leader. He chose to invite the Baghdad government, under Saddam Hussein, to send troops into Kurdistan. The great enemy that the Kurds had spent years fighting, and who had massacred so many of them, was invited back into Kurdistan by a man who had spent most of his life fighting against that enemy. To many people at the time, and to many people since then, it was a move that seemed like a betrayal.

It is vital to understand the reasoning behind the decision if we are to understand Masoud Barzani as both a man and as a leader. What would drive a man who had spent much of his life fighting against Saddam Hussein to invite his forces into a region that was only newly autonomous from Iraq?

Loyalty to the KDP, to his family, and his side was one aspect of the answer. All three appeared to be about to be wiped out by the incursion the PUK had brought about. It seemed that Kurdistan was about to become no more than an area controlled directly by Iran, with the KDP's forces wiped out by the incoming forces. The options that appeared available to Masoud Barzani were to sit back and accept that, to attempt to flee with his supporters, to attempt guerrilla war against Iran's forces, or to do the unthinkable and call in Baghdad's army.

We should discuss each of those options to understand why Masoud Barzani chose the last of them. Sitting back and accepting the Iranian incursion was obviously not possible, because Masoud Barzani had no way of knowing how many of his people would be killed or imprisoned in the process. Yes, it is possible that the control exerted by Iran might have been peaceful, but that is not consistent with Iran's actions in its own Kurdish areas, where it has strictly, and violently, repressed any expression of Kurdish separatism.

Even if there were not that threat, we must remember that the traits that had brought Masoud Barzani this far were ones that would not allow him to give up, or to accept defeat in the face of larger forces. If he had been the kind of person to submit when faced with the threat of larger and better armed military forces, Kurdistan's rebellions against Saddam would have ended long before that point. It was simply inconceivable that he could sit back and accept that he and his forces had lost.

Fleeing was a possibility, since it was a tactic that had been used successfully in both Kurdistan's and his family's history previously. He was born, after all, in a period when his father had led the Barzanis away from Iraq in order to keep them safe. His own period as a leader had included the flight of many of his people across the border into Iran in order to protect them from the Anfal.

The problem with this approach was that historically, it had relied on relatively free movement between Iran and Iraq. Those forces fleeing Iran had done so in the direction of Iraq, while those seeking to escape threats in Iraq had typically fled to Iran. Where one or the other was a safe place, it was a valid strategy, but in the midst of the civil war, it had become impossible. It was not safe to flee south into the main body of Iraq, where Kurds were typically not welcome, while Iran was the major threat in this scenario. In theory, it might have been possible to flee through Turkey or Syria, but they had always been quick to close their borders with Kurdistan at any hint of refugees, and were unlikely to be sympathetic to the KDP's situation.

Staying and fighting was another option, but the simple fact was that the KDP's peshmerga forces were outmatched. When the conflict had been just between the KDP and PUK, things had been well balanced, but the addition of soldiers and armaments from Iran made for a conflict that the KDP simply could not hope to win. To stay and fight alone was to risk being wiped out completely.

That left asking Baghdad for assistance, but there were additional, positive, reasons to do so beyond the simple need to survive at all costs. Masoud Barzani was aware, for example, that there were factors that would limit the extent of Baghdad's involvement, including American pressure. That pressure made it unlikely that Iraq would regain control of Kurdistan in the long term, since that would seem to be a breach of the limits they had established in the wake of the first Iraq war. He would also have been aware that the continuing no fly zone would limit the Iraqi army's ability to attack Kurdish populations, taking away what had long been one of their main advantages over the peshmerga in the region.

Ultimately though, the largest factor that would have persuaded Masoud Barzani was his assessment of the likely future for Saddam Hussein. While we should not suggest that he had the kind of perfect knowledge that we now have, we *can* suggest that his years of experience as a leader had given him the understanding with which to assess what might happen next. Already, the signs were there, in the rebellions that had taken place against him even in the south of Iraq, in the first Gulf War, and in the continued antipathy of the Americans and others towards his rule. It seemed clear to him that it was only a matter of time before Saddam's regime was likely to fall. In that case, why not make use of it to preserve Kurdistan? The alternative was risking becoming part of an Iranian led hegemony, while might prove even harder to extract Kurdistan from than Iraq was.

We know the decision that Masoud Barzani made: he called in the Iraqi army to assist the KDP's forces.

That is a decision that has attracted criticism, yet it has also started to attract praise as time has gone on and the long term effects of the move have become apparent. Initially, there were those who called it a kind of betrayal, yet the effect has been to salvage Kurdistan as an independent entity, prevent its absorption into a larger neighbour, and pave the way for its role in the downfall of Saddam.

The most immediate effect of the call for help was an influx of Iraqi troops in a ground offensive that seems to have taken the PUK by surprise. They were pushed out of Erbil, and of all other major Kurdish cities in the initial rush, reversing the gains they had made with the aid of the Iranians. This was done without the addition of air power, since the no fly zone was still in full effect, yet the ground forces proved to be sufficient to force the PUK to pull back and to drive the Iranians out of the conflict. For a brief time, it seemed that the reversal would be so complete as to provide the KDP with full control of Kurdistan's political and economic resources, with full control of Erbil re-established, and the PUK pulling back to Iran.

That did not happen, partly because of American pressure against the presence of Baghdad's troops, and partly because support for the PUK was genuinely embedded around Sulaymaniyah in particular. There, the party was able to push back against displacement, establishing a line of territory that it was able to hold once more, effectively establishing areas of control that persist even today, in spite of the broader basis of Kurdish politics and the establishment of the rule of law. The result was that this phase of the civil war gave way to others, as the PUK re-established itself in its key areas of control, while the KDP became the dominant governing power in much of the region.

Fighting continued on what would have been a smaller scale were it not for one factor: the decision of Turkey to enter the war. Their government decided that the civil war had become a cover for the PKK, which it considered a terrorist group. It became involved in attacks on PUK and PKK positions, only stopping after American pressure was brought to bear.

The sides engaged in unilateral ceasefires towards the end of 1997, although it took another year for this to be formalised in a treaty between the two sides, brokered by the USA. One side effect of the treaty was the oil for food programme, and the effects of this should not be underestimated, as it provided legitimate avenues for the sides to sell Kurdistan's natural resources, rather than fighting over illicit trade routes. Masoud Barzani played a key role in these negotiations, helping to secure resources for those areas under KDP control, while being willing to stick to the peace deal that was produced, and having sufficient authority to persuade others within his party to do so.

The after effects of the civil war have been considerable. Although it did not result in destruction on the same scale as the Anfal, it has produced knock on political effects that persist to this day. Kurdistan remains effectively divided, with specific areas under the influence of the KDP and PUK. Its rebuilding efforts were hampered by the war, but then financed by the oil for food scheme that came in its wake. The civil war confirmed leaders like Masoud Barzani as both strongly influenced by the conflicts of the past, but also able ultimately to work with other parties to provide benefits for the people of Kurdistan as a whole.

Without the civil war, Kurdistan would be a very different place, politically and culturally. The norms of political life would not be the same, and nor would the ways in which Kurdistan operates through a mixture of official and unofficial channels. Masoud Barzani's role in the conflict is undeniable. He made crucial decisions that led to the preservation of Kurdistan as an independent region, rather than it being subsumed into the Iranian political sphere.

Crucially, these decisions meant that Kurdistan was in a position to take advantage of the situation when, in 2003, Saddam Hussein fell from power in Iraq.

CHAPTER EIGHT

The Overthrow of Saddam

I N THE WAKE of the Civil War, Baghdad had a level of influence again in Kurdistan. It was still not as great as it had been during the 1980s, and Kurdistan remained significantly independent in some respects, but it was still more than it had been in the early 1990s. Baghdad's officials were in control, with its troops and police on the street. The only things stopping massive violence from returning to Kurdistan were the presence of increased international scrutiny, Kurdistan's politicians were no longer able to set its direction, and it was clear that it was not independent in the way that it had briefly been. It was a part of Iraq again for the time being, and at the time, it must have seemed like a disaster to all involved.

As noted in the previous chapter, though, Masoud Barzani was taking a calculated risk in involving Baghdad in Kurdistan's affairs. The calculation was that the situation in Iraq was inherently unstable, and that in just a few years, Saddam would fall either to internal insurrection or external forces. There were good reasons for that calculation, as Iraq had already seen rebellions that had gone far beyond Kurdistan. Equally, there was the pressure of the embargo around Iraq, making conditions there worse and making it more likely that there would ultimately be a change of regime.

By the turn of the millennium, the peace agreement between the PUK and KDP meant that Kurdistan was effectively split into two autonomous regions. The KDP under Masoud Barzani effectively ruled the space around Erbil, while Sulaymaniyah was the PUK's. There were municipal elections in those regions in 2000 and 2001, producing the expected overwhelming support for the parties in question.

At the same time, the international community was putting increasing pressure on the Baghdad regime. There had been intermittent air strikes and sanctions since the first gulf war, with the obvious aim of creating circumstances that would result in an uprising within Iraq. As noted previously, this had actually been stated openly at the end of the first gulf war, with a call for an uprising by the US that ultimately fell short of succeeding. The US, in particular, felt that the conditions existed for further attempts, and that eventually, one of those attempts would succeed. It was a strategy by which they sought to achieve their aims through proxies, and one that should be familiar to any student of the Kurdistan region.

There were more intense periods of air strikes in 1998 and 2001, which may have given Masoud Barzani good reasons to believe that the Baghdad regime would be about to fall. There was an issue, however, in that each side seemed to be hoping that the other would resolve the situation for them. Masoud

Barzani had the willingness, but not the men or the weaponry, while Kurdistan's international partners had the means, but not the willingness.

One key change in this situation came with the September 11th attacks of 2001 on the World Trade Centre. This may not seem immediately relevant to Iraq, as Al Quaeda were never based there, but it is important, because the attack sparked a new willingness in the American government to intervene in the world after years of holding back from any potential loss of American lives. Suddenly, America was willing to use force abroad in a way that it hadn't been willing to do openly for a decade.

The build up to the 2003 invasion of Iraq was slow, and is probably best dated to George W Bush's 'Axis of Evil' speech in 2002. From that point, it seemed clear that, for Masoud Barzani, it involved discussions with Kurdistan's other parties to try to present a unified front when it came to the invasion that they all knew was coming. By late 2002, excuses were being found for the war to come, based on the presence of certain extremist groups (which weren't linked to Al Quaeda directly, but could be), and the supposed presence of weapons of mass destruction. The failure to find these in the wake of the war have made some commentators suggest that there were never any there, but the truth is more nuanced. The people of Kurdistan can attest to Baghdad's use of chemical weapons due to their use during the Anfal and the Iran-Iraq war. They have borne the brunt of such weapons, and while the attack on Halabja was the most famous example, it happened throughout Kurdistan as part of the repeated attacks on villages throughout the region. The failure to find them later suggests, rather, that the regime destroyed or sold such weapons in order to try to take away the excuses the international community might have to act against it.

Those discussions came in 2002, and would eventually lead to a joint leadership in 2003 involving the KDP and PUK. That willingness to work with his political opponents has been a mark of Masoud Barzani's leadership, and in this case, it was a crucial component in Kurdistan's future. Had it not been able to present itself as a single, unified region at this point, it might well not have been the autonomous region that it ended up as.

The discussions were initially aimed at there being a northern front to the war that was to come, but it was limited in scope because of the need for cooperation with Turkey, which refused to allow US forces to travel through it. Kurdistan also suffered protests when it was rumoured that Turkish troops might be coming south to help with the conflict, in a way that ignored Kurdistan and Turkey's history of violence.

The northern front of the war did eventually open up, however, after the beginning of the invasion of the south by the US and the bombardment of positions held by Saddam's troops. Attempts to retake Erbil began in March 2003, with KDP peshmerga forces under Masoud Barzani's direction helping in the conflict to regain Kurdish control over the city.

The actual invasion of Iraq by the US led coalition was relatively brief, with the regime's forces unable to stand up directly to the superior firepower of the coalition forces. This initial phase lasted barely a month, and quickly led to the collapse of the regime's ruling structures, along with the conventional military forces of Iraq.

In this phase, Kurdistan had a smaller role to play as a partner to the coalition than expected, because of Turkey limiting the role of the northern route in the assault. Many US troops were actually a little surprised to find friendly faces waiting for them in Kurdistan, after some of the hostility that they had faced in the south.

There were reasons for the speed of the invasion's success. Superior arms and armaments had a role to play, but so did poor morale among Iraqi army units and high levels of interference from political figures without a real understanding of what to do in the face of such a conflict.

In May 2003, President George W Bush declared an end to major ground operations, effectively suggesting that the job was done, yet history has shown that it was only the beginning. The collapse of the regime's structures created the conditions for an insurgency that spread through Iraq, and for continuing casualties.

While it is necessary to tell this part of Iraq's story in order to understand this period of Masoud Barzani's life, it is also important that we do not make this about the story of Iraq. Instead, we must consider what things would have been like for Masoud Barzani, and for Kurdistan, in this period.

There would have been hope, of course. For so long, Kurdistan's strategy for securing independence had rested on the effects of international partners who had been unwilling to intervene before. Now, those same international partners were actively trying to overthrow the regime that had oppressed them for so long. Masoud Barzani must have felt for a moment that this was an opportunity to change everything for the better. It was why he was so quick to cooperate with the US led joint leadership, and why Kurdistan's peshmerga were ready to join the fight in the chaos that followed.

There would also have been concerns, though, about the things that the invasion might provoke. Looking back, it is easy to see the invasion as the almost inevitable procession towards victory that it became, yet we must remember that in the lead up, no one could have been certain that it would play out that way. I am not suggesting that it was ever likely that Saddam's forces would win outright, but there *was* the risk that things might end up like the previous Gulf War, with the conflict dragging out until the US lost the desire to continue the fight and withdrew. In such circumstances, there was a real risk of acts of retaliation by the regime against all those who had supported the invasion. Even knowing this risk Masoud Barzani judged that it was better to be a part of it than not.

As the invasion took place, and the Ba'athist system started to fall apart, leaving chaos in its wake, the primary concern for Masoud Barzani was to maintain stability within Kurdistan. There were potential risks of Iraqi forces being driven north by the invasion from the south, and that would come from the removal of existing structures of government, with the removal of Ba'athist officials from posts throughout Iraq.

In this, Masoud Barzani was able to demonstrate a clear distinction between Kurdistan and Iraq. He and others were able to do more than just maintain order within Kurdistan: they were able to keep it running, in ways that Iraq as a whole could not. They were able to create a relatively safe, relatively stable Kurdistan in the middle of a period when Iraq as a whole was in turmoil.

This was important for the people of Kurdistan, as it was the first moment when they had a truly safe place, after years of thinking that at any moment the regime might attack. Yet it was even more important in some ways for Kurdistan's relations with the outside world. In a moment of international crisis, with the eyes of the world's press upon Iraq, Masoud Barzani was able to show people that Kurdistan could offer stability in a way that Baghdad could not.

That may not seem like a large thing, but it has been crucial in the years that have followed, for a number of reasons. First, while Kurdistan has always been separate in the eyes of its people, it was one of the first moments when Kurdistan was able to demonstrate that separation in a clear way to people around the world. Previously, Kurdistan was something known about by a few people, and if anyone did know it, it was as a place where a genocide had happened. Now it was referred to in news reports around the world, and in a positive way.

It was also the moment in which Kurdistan effectively 'built its brand', as a relatively stable, reasonable place, with more of a commitment to democracy and rights than the countries around it. It made it clear even before the invasion that it was willing to work with Western partners in a way that somewhere else might not have been. It created a clear impression in one moment, and that impression lasted, so that its Western partners were prepared to give it more of a seat at the international table, and were prepared to start investing in it in return for assistance in managing the chaos that followed.

By providing stability in that moment, Masoud Barzani did more than protect his people during a time of unrest; He created the conditions for the Kurdistan that was to follow, and the Kurdistan that we have today.

A New Start

Once the regime that had controlled Iraq and Kurdistan for so long fell, there was a chance that there had not been for at least a decade, for a completely new start for Kurdistan. It was a moment that had more possibilities contained within it than at any other point. Indeed, in a lot of ways, this was a chance that Kurdistan had never had before, because now it seemed that it would never have to face the threat of heavy handed control from Baghdad again. As we know from events of the last few years, that did not ultimately prove to be the case, but the optimism at that point must have been palpable.

There is a space here in Masoud Barzani's time line between the fall of Saddam's regime in 2003 and his formal election as Kurdistan's president in 2005. We could see this space as simply a gap, but it also seems that important things were happening during this time, and that Masoud Barzani was involved in crucial ways in these events.

The first thing that happened immediately after 2003 was that decisions needed to be made about the shape that things would take in the aftermath of the war. Part of the process of making these decisions was the formation of a ruling council including leaders from the various factions within Iraq and

Kurdistan. As someone who had been involved from the start in the discussions over the invasion, Masoud Barzani had put himself in a position to be involved in the decisions to be made after it. It meant that when the coalition led by the Americans put together a ruling council to maintain stability in Iraq and determine the future shape of its political climate, Masoud Barzani was one of four Kurdish figures who was included. It meant that he was in a position to do more good than he had been able to do in years of opposition to the regime.

The presence of Masoud Barzani on the Iraqi governing council along with others meant that he had a say in the production of Iraq's new constitution, and seems to have played a key role in ensuring that it contained clauses protecting rights, based in part on his experiences of what it is like to have those rights taken away. Although the Baghdad government has not maintained those rights, it says something important about Masoud Barzani that he sought to include them in the first place.

This was also a moment when Masoud Barzani was able to push for the recognition of Kurdistan's status as somewhere separate, and as somewhere that had its own systems, its own economy, and its own policies in many cases. There were limitations to this, of course, because the representatives on the Iraqi side pushed back against the idea of Kurdistan as separate and the Americans weren't willing to contemplate what they saw as further disruption. That meant that instead of full independence, it was only possible for Masoud Barzani to help bring about partial autonomy within the context of a federal system.

Yet this still represented far more formal autonomy than had been the case before, and the circumstances of Iraq meant that there was substantial capacity for informal disruption, allowing Kurdistan the space in which to operate independently on a de facto level.

In the period immediately after 2003, Masoud Barzani was effectively forced to share power with Jalal Talabani of the PUK. His decision to side with the Americans in the name of 'stability' was crucial to the decision to keep Kurdistan within Iraq at the point when it probably had the best chance to break free. It made for a fraught working relationship, especially when they had been on opposite sides of Kurdistan's civil war such a short time before.

As seems to be a familiar pattern in Kurdistan, the two sides mostly settled on running things in their own areas during this period. The familiar divisions of the past manifested themselves in the desire to do the best they could for the cities that were already under their control. At the same time though, they found themselves having to work towards unified political structures for Kurdistan, including a functioning parliament. This level of division would continue until Jalal Talabani went to Baghdad to become President of Iraq in 2005.

In the meantime, we must remember that things were far from peaceful in Iraq. The fall of Saddam led to a multi-sided conflict, where numerous smaller factions were fighting to advance their interests, to push out what they saw as a hostile invasion, or to get revenge for the sudden overturning of a regime that suited them. Even in Kurdistan, it meant attacks such as the 2004 one in Erbil, which led to numerous deaths.

Although the invasion was officially over, the conflict was just beginning, and the chaos caused by it meant that it was impossible to conduct politics as normal, or to run things along the lines that people were used to. Even so, Masoud Barzani made sure that the regions of Kurdistan under KDP control ran smoothly until things settled more, and the situation became more regularised. This was the point where Jalal Talabani's exit to Baghdad allowed for more coherent politics within Kurdistan.

At this point, we must ask why. Why was Masoud Barzani the one left behind in Kurdistan while his great rival there went to become the leader of Iraq? In part, the answer to this is simply one of their degree of cooperation with the objectives of the Americans within Iraq. They wanted someone who was willing to accede to their vision of Kurdistan within a federal Iraq, assuming that their own federal system would be suitable for everywhere else. While both parties in Kurdistan provided support during the conflict, it was clear that Masoud Barzani was less inclined to provide support that would lead to a stronger, more centralised Iraq during times of peace, because that was at odds with the need to break free from that central control.

The second reason was simpler: Masoud Barzani's focus at that point was not on Iraq, but on Kurdistan. While his rivals played the game of trying to be the most important force in Iraq, his attention was on actively helping the people of Kurdistan, trying to help them to recover from both the war and from the years of oppression that had preceded it. He understood in that phase that the most important thing was to build Kurdistan's strength for itself, rather than relying on Baghdad for everything.

Yet it is important to understand that this choice had implications for the future. There were both benefits and drawbacks. The benefits were clear at the time. The more limited engagement with Baghdad gave Masoud Barzani a much greater opportunity to influence events within Kurdistan, and gave him the ability to speak on behalf of Kurdistan much more effectively. It meant that he could work to increase the separation from Baghdad on symbolic, economic, political and military levels in ways that he might not have if he had been intimately bound up with the Iraqi government. On a political level, as the leader left behind, it also meant that he was able to act effectively unopposed within Kurdistan, with many of the internal conflicts that had gone before resolved by default.

The disadvantages came through a reduced ability to influence decisions made in Baghdad, which was important as for large periods, Baghdad has continued to be an important place for Kurdistan, enacting laws and making international agreements that potentially bind it, while having direct control over economic issues such as the release of funds to Kurdistan. The ultimate expression of this came in 2017, with the referendum that led to Masoud Barzani's resignation as Kurdistan's president. It was a situation in which Masoud Barzani had absolute support for both the referendum and independence within Kurdistan, yet had very limited support outside it, particularly within Baghdad. Because there was little influence within Baghdad in the previous fifteen years, nothing had happened to bring the Baghdad government around to the idea that such a thing was necessary or desirable. There had not been the chance to make the legal moves required to allow for the referendum, with the result that Baghdad would be able to frame putting down the referendum as a legal issue aimed at maintaining stability.

Yet what would have happened if Masoud Barzani had gone to Baghdad? Probably, the rate of recovery for Kurdistan would have been slower. Probably, that recovery would have been more intertwined with the south, because the decisions taken at the local level there would have been more likely to follow that 'whole of Iraq' path. Relations might have briefly been better, but could he really have done enough to persuade Baghdad in that phase? Even if he did, would Kurdistan then have been in a position to sustain itself independently.

That is the trade off that Masoud Barzani would have had to balance. With the way things have played out, Kurdistan has gotten itself into a position where it could easily be independent, but must now find ways to persuade Baghdad that such an outcome would be acceptable, or at least not something to actively stop with military force. It has had to deal with Baghdad withholding money owed to Kurdistan, but has been able to overcome this in part through its own oil sales and concentrating on reducing inefficiency and corruption within public life in Kurdistan.

Ultimately, of course, Masoud Barzani didn't really have a choice. He couldn't have been the one to go to Baghdad without being someone entirely different, and holding a very different set of values about the world. In that period, the Americans wanted someone who would be amenable, and who would work within the system that they were trying to (re)construct. They didn't want someone whose approach was founded on emphasising the divisions between Kurdistan and Iraq.

Yet those very qualities made Masoud Barzani the perfect person to run things. It meant that he would put Kurdistan's interests first, not Baghdad's. It meant that he was prepared to fight against those aspects of the system that attempted to pull Kurdistan further into Baghdad's orbit. It meant that Kurdistan had someone who was entirely focused on it in charge at exactly the moment it needed that to bring about its rebuilding.

Jalal Talabani leaving for Baghdad may have meant that Masoud Barzani had to deal with one of his greatest rivals in a position of authority over Kurdistan, but it also meant that, for the first time, he had relative freedom to act within Kurdistan. It cleared the way for him politically to be a president for the whole of Kurdistan, not just for the parts of it that the KDP controlled.

In 2005, the opportunity he had been waiting for finally came. The parliament of Kurdistan elected Masoud Barzani to be the president of the autonomous region. His transition from freedom fighter to politician was complete.

CHAPTER NINE

President

WITH A PRESIDENCY as long running as Masoud Barzani's, it is difficult to know where to begin. There is a temptation to simply proceed chronologically, listing events as they happened, but that provides only limited scope for analysis, and in any case misses the point. There were distinct strands to Masoud Barzani's presidency, and it seems far more helpful to deal with each of them in turn. In the interests of fairness, and because such things cannot be allowed to stand unanswered, we will address the allegations that have been levelled at Masoud Barzani. Then we will move on to explore his role in rebuilding Kurdistan, in addressing community issues within it, in foreign relations, in relations with Baghdad, in economics, in the war against ISIS, and in dealing with the refugee crisis.

Allegations

The job of president in an emerging democracy is a difficult one; that much is without question. In regions that have freed themselves from dictators, the norms of the democratic process are sometimes not embedded as strongly as in those areas where democracy has a kind of inertia based on the weight of history. It is less obvious to participants in the process that things *must* occur in specific ways, because other ways were the norm much more recently. Often, regions whose parliaments are relatively new are still trying to adjust themselves, or find the most effective way in which to operate.

This is made worse in regions that have known wars, because war tends to demand both actions that would not be taken at other times, and ways of looking at the world that are not appropriate in more peaceful environments. Situations born out of wars tend to create a desire for single, powerful leaders rather than pluralism, a respect for hierarchies rather than the freedom to speak up or question decisions, a tendency to act quickly regardless of damage to smaller groups, and a conflation of the public with the personal.

One of the good points about Kurdistan is that it continues to try to work towards a more open democracy, with respect for the rights of all. Yet a part of this process is that we cannot just ignore allegations that have been made against Masoud Barzani during his time as president. Such things must be addressed in the open, rather than ignored. To do otherwise would be a disservice, not just to Kurdistan's democracy, but to Masoud Barzani's story. It does us no good to tell tales of perfect leaders, because that only lures us deeper into the view that says those leaders are the primary drivers of history, and it potentially keeps many people from learning the full lessons of their lives.

Instead, we must look at their lives warts and all, and seek to understand less positive decisions in their proper context. We have already done some of this in the chapter on the civil war, but now it is important to address some of the issues typically raised against Masoud Barzani in his role as president. Broadly speaking, the allegations made typically fall into one of three groups: allegations of excessively favouring members of his family both politically and financially, allegations of wanting to become a kind of strong man or dictator figure, and allegations that he has used both legal and extra-legal means to silence opponents.

It should be remembered in this that no allegation has ever been proven against President Barzani in a court of law, and as such, they must only remain at the level of an allegation. We must equally state that the former president has denied wrongdoing at every stage of his career, and has distanced himself publicly from many of the allegations. In addition to this, we must acknowledge that there are many people who benefit from damaging the Barzani name, and that propaganda is an established tactic used by many of the KDP's political opponents. This section is not written in an attempt to prove or disprove any of these claims, and is certainly not intended as an attack on the former president, but instead, seeks to better understand why they have been made, and to put them into the context of a life that was often spent fighting against real, dangerous enemies.

With regard to the allegations sometimes made of corruption and nepotism, Masoud Barzani has stated on several occasions that he has not personally profited from his role, and that he wishes to be regarded separately from his family in such matters. His personal home remains a modest one, where many political leaders might have tried to profit from their positions.

There have been allegations that money from oil has gone into Barzani pockets, rather than going through official channels. It is true that there is corruption at many levels of Kurdistan's society. It is equally true that not all oil money can be accounted for neatly.

At the same time, we can see that Kurdistan's political structures are filled with members of the same family, so that his nephew is now the president of Kurdistan, and his son is the prime minister. Other Barzani family members have filled roles throughout the government, so that from outside, it must seem that every role is given based on birth-right rather than political suitability. While there are many other nations where families have carved out dynasties in the political sphere, it is rare to have such complete saturation of a political system by one family in more open and functional democracies, with the result that allegations of nepotism have been levelled.

In addressing these issues, we must understand them in the context of a political system grown from a resistance movement. Masoud Barzani, and his family, spent most of their lives engaged in an armed conflict against larger and better equipped forces, forced to use guerrilla tactics to survive, and forced to act in specific ways in order to succeed.

One of these ways was the creation of power and financial structures outside the norms of the country that was trying to oppress the Kurds. In the period where Saddam's government was actively seeking to kill and imprison the Barzanis, it was necessary to gain funds to continue the conflict illicitly, and it was necessary to have power structures based only around those who could be trusted most completely: family members. That these elements have carried over into Kurdistan as it is now is largely because of how deeply, structurally embedded they are within the KDP. Barzani family members' involvement at every level of government is largely because they were involved at every level of the KDP during the fight against Saddam, and because those who became involved when relatively young are just now hitting the ages where they are coming to be candidates for senior posts.

In addition to this, we must consider the wealth of people from all levels of society who are now starting to break into Kurdish politics. Current MPs include some who were formerly among the poorest in the region, while in the area around Barzan, the traditional home of the Barzani family, none of the local officials are from the family.

Similarly, the wealth of some members of the Barzani family these days might be traced back to their illicit activities to gain funds for the fight during the conflicts they have been involved in, and this wealth has largely just carried over into current times, giving them money to invest in more normal business ventures. We can also say that it is obvious that Masoud Barzani is not profiting from any kind of corruption, given the simplicity with which he lives. Equally, it is notable that Barzani run areas have often benefited from the greatest investment in infrastructure, in ways that would seem unlikely if there were misappropriation of funds.

If there some level of confusion between personal and private finances in the wake of the overthrow of Saddam, it was because investment was secured for Kurdistan's rebuilding and the construction of infrastructure, but it was necessary to funnel that funding through the dominant political groups in each area of Kurdistan. That meant that, in those areas of Kurdistan where the KDP's forces held sway, the KDP, and thus the Barzanis, were the natural ones to manage the distribution of these funds. In some recent instances, such as during the financial crisis, the Barzanis were also instrumental in ensuring that wages continued to be paid, more than paying for any previous shortfall.

Equally, we must point out that, in recent years, President Barzani and his son Masrour Barzani have been active in trying to root out corruption in the Kurdistan region. He has cooperated with at least one inquiry into such activities, and has been clear about the threat that it represents to Kurdistan. They have instituted checks on public officials to make sure that they are actually doing their jobs, cracked down on those claiming to hold multiple positions, and on those abusing public funds designed for the widows of martyrs.

There are other allegations, of course. When it comes to the allegations of silencing political opponents, we must be clear about the serious nature of some of these claims. There have been claims in the past that journalists have been killed after criticising the Barzanis, such as over the sequestration of oil funds, that at least one government official has been killed over threatening to uncover embezzlement, that minority Turkmen groups have been attacked, and that political opponents have been subjected to violence. There are accusations relating to Kurdistan's level of press freedom, with suggestions that journalists are harassed by security forces, threatened with imprisonment under libel laws, and placed in a position where it is dangerous to write anything critical of the government.

However, we must ask: in what forum are these criticisms being made? It is in the press. In surrounding regions, where there is a true lack of press freedom, even this would be enough to place people in danger. In Kurdistan though, there is considerable freedom to criticise the government, and it seems that Masoud Barzani's critics often don't care if the allegations are true or not. Simply, Kurdistan is better than most of the places around it, suggesting a willingness to work towards better conditions on Masoud Barzani's part. It is more democratic, less corrupt, and generally freer than most of the neighbouring areas. It is also fair to say that many of the allegations relate to circumstances some years ago, after which the situation has changed considerably.

We must turn to the third general category of allegations: that Masoud Barzani has exhibited some strongman tendencies, including a refusal to truly relinquish power in accordance with Kurdistan's constitution. Such accusations have been levelled at him for some time, initially by those who felt that his presidential term should not have been effectively 'reset' by the creation of Kurdistan's constitution. More recently, those accusations gained more traction, as President Barzani went over his statutory term of office when the conflict against ISIS made it impossible to safely hold elections. This seems a reasonable argument, as far as it goes, although the result was the fragmentation of Kurdistan's political system and greater conflict with its other parties.

We can say that Masoud Barzani has moved on from the presidency. His current role is less defined, as he is still nominally the head of the KDP and the peshmerga. These are, however, designed as temporary measures, aiming to allow continuity in a period where Kurdistan still faces many threats. We must also remember that stepping down as president does not come with a requirement to cease to be a public figure, and that the respect that Masoud Barzani has built up means that in a time when much of Iraq is in conflict with itself, he remains a popular figure. It is said that even protesters elsewhere have called for him to come and be their president, given the current chaos in Iraq.

We must also remember that Masoud Barzani has done nothing to disrupt the political system of Kurdistan since stepping down. The new president still has all of the role's powers, and the parliament still functions as normal. Kurdistan operates mostly through its established channels; it is simply that the times also require the functioning of informal patterns of authority in order to overcome the challenges posed by an unstable Iraq.

After all that he has been through in his life, there can be little doubt that Masoud Barzani is committed to democracy. It seems clear that the long term plan for Kurdistan is for it to be a fully functioning democratic state, but it seems just as clear that this can only happen once Kurdistan is independent. In the meantime, it exists in a region that often does not default to democratic norms, and where personal prestige is often respected more than the rule of law. In this, it is reasonable to question Masoud Barzani and other public figures, but it is also important to remember that he helped to create the conditions in which it is possible to do so.

Rebuilding

One core part of Masoud Barzani's presidency has been the rebuilding of Kurdistan in the wake of the violence that preceded it. The attacks by Saddam, and then the civil war, served to do untold damage to the region. By the time that Kurdistan was settled again in the aftermath of Saddam's fall, almost all of its rural communities had been destroyed, along with what infrastructure it had. It possessed no real connections to the outside world beyond the lines used to smuggle oil across its borders, and had suffered damage to its food systems, its security, and its social structures.

Obviously, these were things that took a whole society to start to rebuild, but we cannot underestimate the role that Masoud Barzani played in that process. It was a process that was essentially funnelled through either the KDP or Kurdistan Regional Government, depending on which sources of funding were used, and Masoud Barzani was the key figure in both, and while he was not the only figure involved in deciding where funds were spent, he did help to make key decisions that resulted in major reshaping of Kurdistan.

Part of this was the rebuilding of Erbil, particularly focusing on the construction of new infrastructure. The KDP focused on trying to improve things in its heartlands, building roads, libraries, and hospitals. In fact, this was a phase when Kurdistan's parties essentially competed to do the most for those in the areas that they controlled. There are, as noted above, those who might consider this parochialism, but it was the only way that Kurdistan could operate for a long time. *Because* there wasn't the infrastructure in place to do things in a more structured way, it was not only necessary, but actively helpful to do things in this way.

The rebuilding had to start with some of the most basic elements: roads and buildings. As part of that, Kurdistan needed money, and Masoud Barzani was one of the key drivers of the region continuing to bring in revenue through its oil resources. Without his international connections, and without the earlier grey market efforts of the region's political parties, it might not have been possible for the Kurdistan Regional Government to establish lasting connections in oil extraction that allowed it to fund this process. He was also crucial in attracting partners in the rebuilding, opening Kurdistan up to outside investment and attracting international backers for the building work. Of course, without Masoud Barzani, we cannot say that it would not have gone ahead anyway. Perhaps some other figure would have helped Kurdistan to find ways to fund its rebuilding, but we *can* say that the process happened faster because he was there. Kurdistan's destruction was almost absolute, and yet in less than a decade, it had bounced back almost completely.

The low level infrastructure of roads and buildings was crucial, but it is probably the larger projects that Masoud Barzani will be remembered for more. In his period as president, Kurdistan acquired crucial public institutions such as libraries and hospitals, and it was his emphasis on helping all of those within the region that ensured that this happened, rather than leaving such things to private providers. Even more importantly, Masoud Barzani's tenure saw the development of Kurdistan's first new universities.

Why was this important? Because for Kurdistan to thrive, it was not enough for it simply to have places for its inhabitants to exist or businesses for them to work in; it had to give them ways to thrive culturally and explore the region's sense of identity. The first university, in Dohuk, was not just about the prestige that came from having such an establishment, but was also about rebuilding Kurdistan on an intellectual level. The earlier attacks on Kurdistan hadn't just destroyed buildings and killed people; they had sought to wipe away all traces of a Kurdish identity.

That made the university important, but also made it vital that the KRG, under Masoud Barzani, should engage in cultural projects. That is why they started to provide funding for a variety of cultural outputs, from writing, to music, to cultural history. The result was not just the preservation of a Kurdish identity, but the construction of one aimed at the whole of Kurdistan, one that sought to welcome all elements of its communities together.

Of course, one rebuilding project stands out above all of the others as a symbol of the new Kurdistan: its first international airport, in Erbil. Such a thing would have been inconceivable in the days that had gone before; indeed, in the moments when Kurdistan had seemed starved of allies, it would have seemed that there was no reason for it. Masoud Barzani, however, saw that there *were* reasons for it, and important ones: it provided crucial links to the outside world that did not depend on Kurdistan's land borders; it provided opportunities for wider trade; it provided a way to travel to and from the region without having to pass through the bulk of Iraq or Iran first, helping to establish it as a separate place. Crucially, in the future, it also meant that Kurdistan had sufficient international links of its own to act as a partner to its allies independently of Baghdad in the fight against ISIS. The construction of the airport began in July 2003, and the first flights were landing there just months later. In just two years, Kurdistan had a regular airline running international flights.

This process of rebuilding probably isn't what will get the most attention when we look back on Masoud Barzani's career, yet it *does* deserve at least some attention. It is easy to look at Kurdistan now and forget just how damaged it was at the point when Masoud Barzani became president. He not only helped to bring Kurdistan towards a more independent state; he helped to rebuild it into a safe, modern region suited to the more urban lives that its inhabitants lead today.

Communities and Equality

One key aspect of Masoud Barzani's time as president of Kurdistan has been Kurdistan's movement away from its neighbours on issues of equality and human rights. Many of the nations that surround Kurdistan have longstanding issues with human rights, and significant inequalities on issues of gender, race and religion. These inequalities have often led to violence, to injustices, and to minority groups feeling that they cannot play any full part in the societies in which they live.

Kurdistan has worked to progressively become a more equal society on a number of levels since its establishment as an autonomous region. It has become accepting of minority religious groups, and has consciously provided seats within its parliament for smaller communities within its borders. This has meant guaranteed representation for groups such as Assyrians, and also the religious protection of groups such as Christians and Yazidis, who are often attacked religiously and physically elsewhere.

By far the biggest group to benefit from the development of Kurdistan, however, has been women. While in the past, it could be said that Kurdistan was a strongly patriarchal and sexist society, and while there is definitely still progress to be made, we can also say that it is considerably further along that path than almost anywhere around it. The Kurdistan Regional Government must always have at least a third of its members of parliament be women. Laws have been enacted in Masoud Barzani's time as president to try to eliminate violence against women, and to encourage their greater engagement in public life. During his presidency, levels of female education and freedom within Kurdistan have increased dramatically.

There will be those who will argue that these changes are a reflection of transitions in Kurdistan's society as a whole, and this is true, but it is also true that Masoud Barzani played a specific role in the provision of greater equality within Kurdistan. He was involved in the drafting of Kurdistan's constitution, and thus in the clauses that enshrined so many of the protections for disadvantaged groups. As president, he was also involved in much of the legislation that sought to improve protections for women, and was instrumental in seeking to push their involvement in the police force and armed services. When it came to the war against ISIS, he and others within Kurdistan were the ones who sought to protect the Yazidis, when Baghdad and others were prepared to abandon them.

Throughout his presidency, Masoud Barzani has also stressed his commitment to equality within Kurdistan, to improvements in the democratic process, and to the development of rights within the region. This might seem like a minor thing, but actually, the things that leaders say matter when it comes to the treatment of minorities. Where leaders elsewhere demonise or belittle minority groups, they help to create the conditions in wider society for their mistreatment. Where, as Masoud Barzani has done, those leaders seek to emphasise the role of minority groups within a society, or to stress the important place of women, those groups are more likely to be protected.

In stressing the commitment of Kurdistan to the protection of such groups, Masoud Barzani ensured that others would take the issues involved more seriously. In stressing Kurdistan's commitment to moving towards a truly equal democracy, he created the conditions in which it could. In a society where years of conflict had conditioned people to look to charismatic leaders for direction, the positions that Masoud Barzani chose to take on these issues mattered.

Nor should we see it as an easy thing to do, without consequences. Every society around Kurdistan was, and is, more conservative, with fewer rights for minorities and often open attacks on them. By taking a stance that sought to include those groups, Masoud Barzani essentially created distance between Kurdistan and its neighbours. By not being the same, he created a situation in which Kurdistan could not simply fit in and erase the hate those countries felt for it.

Why did Masoud Barzani choose this stance? In part, of course, it was because there was very little point in trying to fit in. Kurdistan was, and is, separate. The hatred felt towards any expression of that was never going to go away. Equally, by trying to fit in, Kurdistan would have reduced its distinctiveness, the separateness of its culture, and many of the arguments in favour of its independence.

We can also say that this commitment to equality had benefits in terms of its relations with its allies. Western partners and outside investment flocked to Kurdistan under Masoud Barzani's presidency in part because they saw Kurdistan as stable and progressive compared to the societies around it, certainly compared to Iraq as a whole. Its commitment to the protection of minorities definitely played a part in that. Its alliance with Israel, for example, has long been founded on a mutual sense that Israel and Kurdistan have both suffered oppression, and are trying to build better societies in a region that still has much animosity towards them.

Yet to put it like that makes it all sound like no more than a calculated political move, a policy decision that only goes skin deep. It is clearly more than that, when Kurdistan was prepared to risk the lives of its peshmerga to protect Yazidi communities, and when the guaranteed seats in its parliament mean that those communities have a real say in the way that it is governed.

Part of the reason for Masoud Barzani's commitment to equality is because he has experienced being attacked first hand in his life. He has seen what it is like when a larger group targets a smaller one and tries to eliminate them culturally, then physically. Having lived through the Anfal, through the murders of those like him, through the destruction of his people's entire way of life, how could he *not* want to help other communities that found themselves in a similar position. Having grown up under Saddam, how could he not want to ensure that Kurdistan moved forwards towards a society that was freer and more equal?

Foreign Relations

Masoud Barzani's presidency has been marked by a huge increase in Kurdistan's presence on the world stage, and by improved relations with many countries around the world that might not even have known of Kurdistan's existence before, except perhaps through news reports on the Anfal. His presidency has meant a widening of Kurdistan's base of allies, a strengthening of its ties with key friends such as the United States, and even improvements in its relations with neighbours who might in the past have been only too willing to treat it as an enemy.

Kurdistan's relationship with the United States has strengthened under his presidency, with Masoud Barzani and members of the Kurdistan Regional Government making several trips to the US during his presidency. He has met US presidents and received US congressional delegations. In doing so, he has sought to move Kurdistan into the public eye within America, knowing that the USA is a key power broker in wider international relations. He has also sought to change the perception of Kurdistan, which may once have been seen in the US media purely as a region under attack, to being seen as a valued ally.

Masoud Barzani has also improved Kurdistan's relations with its European partners, partly concentrating on the thriving Kurdish communities in many European nations, partly seeking to ensure that Kurdistan has sought as wide a base of international acceptance as possible. In part this was based on a belief that with enough international acceptance of Kurdistan, it might be possible to make the transition to an independent state relatively seamlessly.

Even with the countries around Kurdistan, which have often been prepared to attack it, Masoud Barzani has made an effort to improve relations. Kurdistan's relations with Iran improved considerably for a time under his presidency, to the extent that Iranian funds became a prime source of investment for Kurdish private enterprise. Even with countries such as Turkey, it became possible to at least engage in meaningful trade in oil with them for a time. We cannot say that the animosity involved went away under him, but at least there was a recognition that it was possible to do business.

We can say that Masoud Barzani's foreign relations as president had a number of key strands and approaches to them. One of these was the pragmatism mentioned above. He was willing to do business with anyone, even if they had previously shown themselves to be less than friendly to Kurdistan. Years of being attacked on all sides had taught him to take friends where he could find them, although not to extend more trust than was wise. He was aware that many of the countries around Kurdistan still didn't care whether its people lived or died, but he was at least able to shift many relationships to involve a pragmatic business relationship rather than one involving outright hatred.

A second strand was improving Kurdistan's ability to offer something to the outside world independently from Baghdad. The construction of Erbil's international airport under his presidency was a huge moment in this, since it allowed for the establishment of long distance connections and trade, without being reliant on Kurdistan's land borders. The management of Kurdistan's oil resources was another element of this, as even countries who had no interest in Kurdistan's political situation had an interest in its oil. With the US, a willingness to accept its military during the fight against ISIS and the general breakdown in Iraq also helped to cement relations. Kurdistan made itself useful to the world, and that created diplomatic capital for it.

Another strand of Masoud Barzani's foreign relations was an emphasis on Kurdistan's separateness from Iraq. Even as others around the world sometimes tried to insist on Kurdistan being bundled in with Iraq in international affairs, he sought to emphasise that the Kurdistan Regional Government was something to be addressed separately, and that would not necessarily go along with what was suitable for Baghdad. This was made easier for much of his presidency by a less than stable situation in Iraq, so that Kurdistan often seemed like the only reasonable, safe, stable voice in the region.

The results of this approach can be seen in the startling number of embassies housed in Erbil (from 38 UN nations), who essentially talk to Kurdistan as if it is a separate nation, even if it is yet to achieve that status. The results can also be seen in a generally wider knowledge of Kurdistan as a place worldwide, so that now there are fewer and fewer blank looks when the region's name is mentioned.

A fourth, crucial strand has been the ability of Masoud Barzani and his representatives to find a way into the action of international politics, even when they have not always been invited. There were certainly events in the early days of Kurdistan when Masoud Barzani simply attended, making sure that Kurdistan was not shut out of discussions that should properly involve it. More recently, it has seen Kurdistan invited more officially to international discussions, occasionally on better terms than the Baghdad government has been.

Finally, Masoud Barzani has made efforts to improve Kurdistan's standing within the international media, seeking to ensure that more people hear about it, and that more understand the role it could play within the wider region. That is as important as any of the other strands, since a population that is forgotten is one that is at greater risk.

Of course, we could argue over how effective these measures have proved, given the way the international community largely abandoned Kurdistan in the wake of its referendum. Yet some parts of this, including the relations it had built up, served to limit the extent of Baghdad's retaliation.

More importantly, many of those relationships have persisted, suggesting that they are about more than just one moment. In that, Masoud Barzani has succeeded in producing lasting changes to Kurdistan's international relations, and those changes have generally been to the region's immense benefit.

Relations with Baghdad

Kurdistan's relations with Baghdad have both changed and remained similar under Masoud Barzani. Clearly, things are not quite the same as they were under Saddam Hussein, yet at the same time the relationship is still a frequently hostile one, and the referendum of September 2017 showed that Baghdad was still prepared to use force against Kurdistan.

Let's start with the ways that things changed under Masoud Barzani. Clearly the nature of the relationship shifted, from one where a hostile Baghdad regime was trying to actively murder as many Kurds as possible, to one where even its use of force was limited by pressure from outside, and where more chaotic parts of Iraq have even put out calls for Masoud Barzani to come in and help run them. Both of these point to the ways in which Masoud Barzani has been able to build up the relationship there, even as it has remained a largely hostile one. By building up Kurdistan, both literally through infrastructure and more generally in the eyes of the wider world, he created a situation in which the bulk of Iraq was less able to do as much harm.

Part of this was because Masoud Barzani changed the nature of the relationship between Kurdistan and Baghdad. The Iraqi constitution clearly tries to claim Kurdistan as no more than a semi-autonomous part of it, yet Masoud Barzani stressed this autonomy at every turn throughout his time as president. He also put an effort into building up the administrative, political and military structures of Kurdistan, separately from Baghdad's.

The result was a situation where the two related to one another in ways that were more like state to state relations and less like centre to locality relations. This can be seen in Kurdistan's separate representation at some international events, in its separate involvement in conflicts alongside its own allies, and in the mediated nature of talks between the two.

Of course, it is possible to argue that, to some extent, this situation is simply the result of outside factors and nothing to do with Masoud Barzani. There are probably those who will put it down to the impact of the American no fly zone and the initial uprisings to establish the region's independence, yet we must remember that Masoud Barzani was intimately involved with those as well, earlier in his work. We could argue that this relationship has been the natural consequence of the drive towards independence, yet again we must ask who has been fuelling that drive. Masoud Barzani has, consistently and clearly, throughout his time as president.

There have been obvious strains in the relationship with Baghdad during his tenure, of course, and we should probably address some of the most important issues and flash points.

There were early difficulties with Baghdad over the scope and the detail of the Iraqi constitution, approved in 2005. That constitution sought to set out Kurdistan's place within a broader Iraq, even as it pushed towards greater freedom from it. With outside pressure, particularly from the US, Masoud Barzani and the KRG found themselves pushed into accepting it.

There were also issues once Jalal Talabani became the president of Iraq, its first Kurdish president. In general, that should have been a beneficial moment for Kurdistan, since it meant that the whole of Iraq had a president who understood its concerns, and that was true, certainly compared to some of the presidents who came afterwards, but it also created tensions. One of those tensions was a feeling from the centre that because it had effectively co-opted parts of Kurdistan's politics, it could also take over some decisions relating to it. Masoud Barzani naturally resisted that. There were also some issues that emerged because of the level of personal rivalry that existed between Masoud Barzani and Jalal Talabani. This is probably one instance where Masoud Barzani's presence probably made things worse, because it was impossible for the two to completely put aside their history of conflict as the heads of rival parties. That is not to say that things would necessarily have been better with a different KDP leader, or that there was any way to reasonably resolve it; it is simply important to note that this is one instance where the personalities involved did play a role.

There have been two key flash points since with the Baghdad government. The first was over the issue of who had paid, or not paid, what they should under the Iraqi constitution. The Baghdad government attempted to say that all oil revenues from Kurdistan should be funnelled through it, but the Kurdistan Regional Government did not trust that it would ever see any of those funds again. The KRG, meanwhile, made it clear that Baghdad was not sending north the funding that was mandated under the Iraqi constitution (17% of national revenues). The result was an impasse that Kurdistan was able to sustain for a time, but which quickly became worse due to an escalating war with ISIS and the resulting flow of refugees from Syria.

The result was an economic crisis within Kurdistan which resulted in many less essential government staff not being paid for some time, as priority was given to frontline staff such as the peshmerga. Masoud Barzani was at the heart of the management of this crisis, ensuring that key services continued to run, but also refusing to simply give in to Baghdad's pressure.

The other major point of conflict was over the referendum. This will be discussed in detail in the following chapter, and may be seen by some as the defining moment of Masoud Barzani's presidential career. Briefly, it highlighted that the conflicts with Baghdad had not gone away, and showed that Baghdad was still willing to use force against Kurdistan. Even today, in the aftermath of all these events, there is still political conflict between Kurdistan and Baghdad, which has resulted in the withholding of Kurdistan's mandated 17% of Iraq's tax revenue by Baghdad in an effort to put pressure on the KRG.

These conflicts both showed the extent to which the relationship between Kurdistan and Baghdad can be influenced by individual politicians, and the underlying structural factors that will mean those conflicts continue. As long as Baghdad sees value in the oil within Kurdistan, it will continue to claim ownership over it. As long as it seeks a unified country, it will continue to attack moves towards separation. In those contexts, all a leader can hope to do is manage the impacts of what comes, and we can say that is something that Masoud Barzani succeeded in during his time as president.

The War Against ISIS

One unexpected element that came to be a key concern in the later years of Masoud Barzani's presidency was the war against ISIS. While this group was initially confined to Syria, its activities quickly spread into Iraq as well, making significant gains. Kurdish peshmerga forces have been at the heart of the fight against it.

The rise of ISIS in Syria came in the wake of a failed uprising by Syria's people, which led to the destabilisation of the region and created opportunities for more extreme groups to become a part of the political landscape. The conflict that followed led to rapid gains for ISIS within Syria, including in many of the areas bordering Kurdistan. Although the conflict initially seemed like something that might be confined to Syria, it quickly spread beyond, with Iraq particularly badly hit. Baghdad lost control of a number of key areas near Kurdistan, including the disputed city of Kirkuk. In fact, 'lost control' is too neutral a term; Baghdad abandoned large areas of Iraq's north in order to focus on protecting the zones nearest the capital. At the same time, in 2014, ISIS struck at a number of Kurdistan's areas, taking control of towns such as Sinjar.

It is impossible to overstate the cruelty and violence that followed. Groups such as the Yazidis were particularly persecuted, but there were murders across all communities, and dictatorial rule that made life harder for every person in those areas.

Masoud Barzani was intrinsically involved in the process of the fight back, coordinating with Kurdistan's US allies to ensure that air strikes were used to support peshmerga troops on the ground. The result was that Kurdistan's troops were able to push back ISIS forces even in areas where Baghdad could not, and Kurdistan was able to free groups who might otherwise have been killed. Its peshmerga, normally deployed only within Kurdistan's limits, had to push forward to protect a larger area than usual, and did so successfully, when many of those around were still caught up in their own internal conflicts, and outside allies were unwilling to commit troops on the ground, despite the potential threat ISIS posed to the wider world.

In this, we can see echoes of earlier conflicts involving Kurdistan, where its allies have been quick to employ it as a means to fight some other threat, thus sparing them from having to risk their own lives. We can even see echoes of earlier abandonments in what has come next, both in the wake of the referendum of 2017 and in Turkey's attacks on Kurdish positions elsewhere. As in the past, Kurdish fighters have been relied upon to risk their lives, have taken ground from forces that others did not wish to fight, and have then been abandoned to their fate when the countries around them decided that they had no wish to allow any kind of Kurdish territory near them.

Put like that, there is an argument for not becoming involved in other people's conflicts, yet Masoud Barzani did, and it was undoubtedly the correct decision. There are a number of reasons for this. One is moral. It is inconceivable that anyone could stand by and allow others to suffer as people were suffering under ISIS. Just because other nations were willing to stand by, or run away, that doesn't mean that Kurdistan should have. Having suffered attempted genocide, the people of Kurdistan were more willing to fight against such attacks on others, and Masoud Barzani in particular was not willing to stand by.

Secondly, there were pragmatic reasons: Kurdistan was just as much under attack as anyone else. Had it not joined the fight, it would have been alone against the threat. By committing Kurdistan's troops in coordination with its international allies, Masoud Barzani was able to ensure that air support was available for the peshmerga's actions, and that they were resupplied with weaponry.

Third, we cannot deny that the fight provided Kurdistan with opportunities to expand its reach in the region. Because Baghdad had abandoned control over Kirkuk, for example, the peshmerga's retaking of it both denied ISIS valuable resources in the form of oil and secured the city for Kurdistan. The phase before Baghdad's retaking of Kirkuk in the wake of the 2017 referendum was probably the largest that Kurdistan had been for hundreds of years.

At the very least, it provided Kurdistan with the chance to demonstrate its reliability as an international partner, its stability in an unstable region, and its ability to function independently from a Baghdad that was in disarray.

What though, were the consequences of the war against IS? In part, we can say that it helped to bring about the referendum that followed, creating conditions for it when they might otherwise not have existed. It helped to convince Masoud Barzani that a similar moment would not come again. It also helped to create instability in Iraq that survives to this day, so that Kurdistan remains relatively stable in comparison. It helped to created opportunities for Kurdistan, but also created a back-lash against its perceived expansion, and the chaos created opportunities for its enemies to strike out at it. Kurdistan found that the international community's aversion to further disruption meant that it would not support Kurdistan in its push for independence, and it meant that Masoud Barzani did not have as many opportunities available to him as he may have perceived.

There were other consequences, too, with the disruption of economic activity, and the perception that the whole region was unsafe to do business in. The taking of Kirkuk meant a brief boost to Kurdistan's oil income, but the costs of war may have ultimately outweighed this.

This is particularly true when we consider one key effect for Kurdistan during the conflict with ISIS, which was the influx of refugees. Masoud Barzani's presidency might not be remembered for his handling of this situation in the same way as the referendum, but it was just as crucial, and showed key aspects of his approach.

Refugees

The conflict in Syria, first as an uprising against its government, then as an ongoing battle against ISIS, resulted in significant changes to the political landscape around the world. The so called 'Arab Spring' of attempted revolutions that sparked it caused what has come to be called 'the migrant crisis' globally. Suddenly, people were fleeing conflict zones in multiple countries, with a resulting rise in the number of refugees and other migrants. This rise came as a shock to many countries, with the result that they suddenly had to confront their approach to refugees, immigration, and the impact of their actions on a global scale.

In some countries, the crisis triggered a retrenchment, with immigration growing as a political issue, resulting in the election of more right wing, anti-immigrant parties in the US and much of Europe. There, the crisis (mixed in with the earlier global financial crisis), effectively burst the bubble of more progressive, third way politics founded on a mixture of free market globalisation and social progressiveness. When countries like Sweden and Germany declared their openness to refugees, and tried to demand that others follow suit, it merely made the countries on the way to them close themselves off harder in response.

What all of these far off countries failed to understand though was that, for every one refugee who made it across the world to somewhere like Northern Europe, there were dozens more who fled the shortest distance possible, to the countries immediately surrounding Syria. Some, like Turkey, took in hundreds of thousands, but only after promises from Europe to pay for them (and thus slow the onward flow). Yet for those Syrians of Kurdish descent, it seemed that there was one obvious place to run: Kurdistan.

The result was that more than 300,000 people crossed the border into a region with a population of at most eight million. That meant that, in the course of just months, one in every thirty people within Kurdistan was a refugee. It was a massive change for such a small region, and especially the region around Erbil, whose population currently stands at around

850,000 people, after an increase of more than a hundred thousand refugees.

The Syrian refugees were not the only ones; many Iraqis found themselves pushed north due to instability within the south of Iraq, but initially they were not counted in the same tallies that the Syrians were, as in the eyes of the international community they had not crossed a border. We know, for example, that, while there are only ten refugee camps for the Syrian refugees (holding perhaps 90,000 of them, with the rest distributed among the population), there are more than forty for internally displaced Iraqis. In total, it is estimated that more than 1.5 million refugees and internally displaced people are included in the 8.39 million population of Kurdistan, or more than one in eight.

That is a huge change as a percentage of population at the best of times, yet we also have to remember that these were anything but the best of times for Kurdistan. It was a period when the region was suffering economic difficulties, in large part due to the actions of the Baghdad government. It was also a period when it was itself under attack by ISIS, having to pour its efforts into the peshmerga in an attempt to survive the conflict. Kurdistan was also, certainly initially, the recipient of far less international funding to support its intake of refugees than places like Turkey, simply because the funding to Turkey was intended as a kind of bribe to keep refugees away from Europe.

In such circumstances, it might have been forgiven if Masoud Barzani had taken the approach favoured by others in the region at times when Kurdistan's people had needed to flee: closing the borders. Certainly, some other areas were far less welcoming to refugees, with Iraq initially building no refugee camps at all. Yet the same arguments apply that came into play with Kurdistan's involvement in the war against IS: after all that had happened to the people of Kurdistan in the past, after all the times that he and those around him had been forced to flee across borders in order to be safe, Masoud Barzani could not stand by while others found themselves forced from their homes. This was particularly true for other groups of Kurds, many of whom found themselves shut out by regimes that were prepared to take in anyone else but them.

In keeping with Kurdistan's traditions of hospitality, and because he was aware that action was needed urgently, Masoud Barzani initially encouraged the acceptance of refugees into the local population, and then sought to bring about the building of suitable refugee camps for those who could not be housed elsewhere. It was difficult, when there was not the funding in place to do it, but part of what Masoud Barzani did as president was to seek such funding from international organisations, encouraging them to become involved and reminding them of Kurdistan's important role in such a humanitarian emergency. The result was that, while the situation was anything but easy, it was possible for Kurdistan to support even such a huge influx into its population.

Doing so demonstrated both Masoud Barzani's ability to obtain international support for his actions and his willingness to simply act when he saw that it was necessary to do so. There are plenty of other leaders who might have waited, or who might have said that because no one helped Kurdistan on many previous occasions, there was no reason for it to help others now. Instead, he set out a framework for it to bear its share and more of the burden, potentially saving many thousands of lives. Even today, fresh refugees are arriving in Kurdistan from Syria, largely as a result of Turkey's attempts to push out any Kurds they find there. Kurdistan continues to be a safe haven for them, largely thanks to the initiatives that Masoud Barzani put in place.

Under another leader, those refugees might still have come, but we have seen from other countries in the region that it would not have been automatic that they would have been protected. Several neighbouring countries made a point of closing their borders in the face of the refugee crisis, and have put little provision in place to look after the refugees involved. Turkey has threatened on several occasions to simply drive displaced individuals on towards other countries. Masoud Barzani did neither of those things. Instead, he sought to help those who needed it, regardless of where they were from, and regardless of the cost.

That cost is something we must discuss, though, along with other economic factors, because the economics of Masoud Barzani's presidency had a direct influence on the lives of those within Kurdistan.

Economics

Kurdistan's economy has been in a complex position through much of its existence. In being ruled over by others, it essentially became an economy designed for the benefit of those who colonised it. In the twentieth century, it made moves from an agrarian economy to an essentially oil based one, but still, the benefits of that economy were turned outward. First, the British took the profits from the oil, and then Baghdad did.

At the point when Masoud Barzani became president, the situation was more mixed. Formally, all oil revenues were still meant to go to Baghdad, but the limitations imposed by previous oil embargoes and the need to feed the people of the region meant that black market routes had already been set in place to bring revenue into the region directly.

As time went on, the trade in oil was put on a more formal footing, with the stability of the region creating conditions in which it was possible for major oil companies to do business. The resulting funds were the ones needed to start to rebuild Kurdistan, to pay for its peshmerga and its infrastructure. The trade has been central to Kurdistan's economy, and Masoud Barzani played a key role in ensuring that trade worked for the benefit of Kurdistan, rather than Baghdad.

For a while, it seemed as though this might be enough. Kurdistan had oil revenues, and was supposedly guaranteed an income from Iraq's overall tax revenues. It even started to pull in a small amount of outside investment, as other countries saw opportunities in the one region of Iraq that was relatively safe and open for business. The scale of the funds available can be seen in the rebuilding explored earlier, in Kurdistan's construction of new buildings and roads, its universities and its airport. For a while, it seemed that Kurdistan's economy was booming.

Yet there were economic problems on the horizon, even built into the system that Kurdistan found itself a part of. There were key structural issues that Masoud Barzani needed to address. One was the reliance on funds that were supposed to come up from Baghdad, but which it began to withhold as arguments with Kurdistan intensified.

This withholding was not necessarily a problem in itself, because it just meant that Kurdistan ceased to transfer any oil revenues southward, instead relying on them to fund its burgeoning state. That intensified the breakdown of relations with Baghdad, as seen above, but it had a more serious economic knock on effect for Kurdistan by making it in effect a mono-culture. In spite of the attempts of the KRG, the economy was not heavily diversified, largely because it takes time to do that, building up a stock of higher technology industries only once sufficient people have been through Kurdistan's universities. Heavy industry would require considerably greater connections to the outside world, and probably a larger population. That left Kurdistan worryingly dependent on its oil revenues, especially since it was a system without direct taxation.

This could have been acceptable, had oil prices remained high. In 2014, though, the price of oil crashed, partly due to increased supplies elsewhere, partly because of increases in US production that reduced its need for outside oil. The result was that Kurdistan's revenues fell abruptly. This would have been bad enough, but Kurdistan also found itself faced with a number of other issues. The refusal of Baghdad to pay its mandated share of tax revenues was one issue, but there were also massively increased costs due to the difficulties involved in the war against ISIS, and due to the numbers of refugees driven out of surrounding regions by that conflict. One of these factors alone would have been difficult, but the combination of them all was devastating. From a position where it had been able to invest heavily within Kurdistan, suddenly, the government didn't have the money to pay the wages of those involved in public service.

In most countries, this would have been a serious issue; in Kurdistan, it was a potential disaster, because of the high proportion of jobs in the public sector there. Overnight, civil servants and officials were not being paid their full salaries, and in some cases were not being paid at all. This was happening in the middle of an armed conflict where failing to pay soldiers or provide food for refugees might result in many thousands of deaths. Masoud Barzani had to start to make difficult decisions as the government's revenues fell, first by prioritising the pay of the peshmerga who defended Kurdistan over other groups, then by trying to work out ways to both limit the government's outgoings and maximise its income.

This prioritisation of the peshmerga was made necessary by the Baghdad government's refusal to provide funding for Kurdistan's military forces. Baghdad has long held that Kurdistan, as one of 'its' regions, should not have separate military forces. That meant that the KRG had to find funding for its troops through internal means.

Dealing with corruption within the region was one method, with Masoud Barzani seeking to eliminate cases of people drawing multiple salaries for the same work, or being paid for sinecures where they did little to no work. The issue of fake war widows was addressed, with there being more widows on pensions for fallen soldiers than there had ever been soldiers. Officials in public life started to have their hours checked and their performances reviewed. These might all sound like simple, obvious things once they are in place, but they are things that took real force of personality and trust from the population to bring about.

It was also necessary, however, to divert funds from other ministries. This was painfully reminiscent of so called 'austerity' programmes elsewhere in the world, where potential lenders on the international markets try to force an agenda of cuts through states with a large public sector, rather than trying to stimulate growth. In the short term, it might have been necessitated by the war, but in the longer term, it is not a path consistent with Kurdistan's values.

A partial recovery started to take place as the situation stabilised, but Kurdistan's economy was weakened somewhat by the crash. Worse, the recovery was built on essentially the same lines as before, with it proving difficult to diversify the economy at any speed in the run up to the referendum. Attempts to bring in more industry foundered the moment the KRG wasn't heavily subsidising it, because the industries concerned decided that they could get a better deal in Baghdad. This seems short sighted, though, because of the greater stability and freedom from violence that Kurdistan offers.

While Masoud Barzani is no longer the President of Kurdistan, he will certainly recognise the pattern that has occurred since February 2020, when the worldwide slowdown sparked by the Covid 19 pandemic caused oil prices to crash. Countries in lockdown were not using even a fraction of the oil that they once were, with the result of a dramatic loss of revenue. This has been compounded by ongoing disputes with Baghdad, resulting in the refusal of the central government to pay out tax revenues. Again, the KRG finds itself faced with hard choices about who it can pay and whose salaries must be reduced, while up to a quarter of a million 'ghost' employees exist on the books, drawing salaries with no pay.

Obviously, the current situation is not down to Masoud Barzani; although he remains involved in the politics of the KDP, he has no direct say over the decisions of the KRG. We must ask though about the phase where he *was* still president, from 2015–2017. Why did nothing change in that time?

The answer is that Masoud Barzani actually took many steps towards comprehensive change. He sought to reduce corruption substantially, and tried to diversify the economy. The failure of these two things came in part from a lack of political unity within Kurdistan, and in part from structural issues so deep that no one could hope to change them. The diversification of an economy, or the transformation of a banking system, is something that takes decades, yet Masoud Barzani found himself forced to attempt both in a matter of a couple of years, while there was a conflict going on around him, and while there was significant political division that was threatening to tear the KRG's structures apart.

Was there anything good to come out of the economic crash of 2015 that might point to better signs for the future? Perhaps we can suggest that the speed of Kurdistan's economic recovery last time round implies that such a thing might be possible again with another upswing in the price of oil. Can such a thing be guaranteed, though, in the long term, especially if the world starts to take the decarbonisation of its economies seriously? Equally, it seems callous to suggest that there was anything good about thousands of people losing their jobs and their incomes. Attempts to force Kurdistan into a smaller public sector created worse working conditions and more difficult lives for its people. What we can say though is that the earlier economic crash had a direct influence over events that were to come, creating the conditions in which people thought that the risk of a referendum was better than the status quo. It showed the people of Kurdistan that the situation with Baghdad was never likely to improve, and that the moment had come to change things. Masoud Barzani took full advantage of that moment.

Success?

It is said that all political careers end in failure, and in general, that is true. If a major event does not bring a halt to someone's political career, then they will simply keep going until stopped by ill health. This is particularly true in the Middle East, where notions of politicians retiring are much less common than elsewhere. In general, in most political systems, a politician will continue until some situation makes it more appropriate for them to step down from their office than not. Typically, this comes when they place all of their existing political In Masoud Barzani's case, this situation was the aftermath of the referendum, where it had seemed that he might finally achieve his dream for Kurdistan, but only if he put everything on the line politically.

It is easy to judge politicians by what brings them down. Many do not escape the stain of whatever finally pushes them from office. Yet sometimes, it is more useful to judge them by the person they were up to that point. To examine the whole of their political career in a balanced way, we must take away our thoughts and feelings about whatever brought it to an end, and explore what they achieved in the period before.

Clearly, Masoud Barzani has achieved much in his life, as a freedom fighter, as a symbol of the push towards independence, and as a bridge between the old and new strands of Kurdistan's political landscape. Yet how successful was he purely as a president? If we take away the referendum, then we can suggest that he was actually fairly successful. Yes, there were issues and allegations that needed to be addressed, but almost uniquely for politicians in the region, he was willing to do so openly. He played a key role in the rebuilding of Kurdistan after the ravages brought about by both Saddam's regime and the civil war. He was instrumental in the development of Kurdistan's institutional structures and norms, actively seeking to cut down on waste and corruption. He helped to create an environment in Kurdistan where the situations of women and minority groups have started to improve, even if to an outside observer it may seem that there is still room for growth.

Crucially, he has brought Kurdistan out into the world. Where his father sought international allies on a purely military basis, Masoud Barzani's position as president meant that he sought to raise Kurdistan's prestige more generally, promoting it as a safe, stable place in which to do business. He was able to attract outside investment, and to secure Kurdistan's seat at the table in international discussions. Even those who might have opposed his moves towards independence cannot deny that by emphasising it, Masoud Barzani helped to create conditions in which international partners took Kurdistan seriously as a separate entity from Baghdad.

Some of his most important moments came in the management of an ongoing crisis with ISIS and Syria, both coordinating the military response and ensuring that the humanitarian crisis that accompanied it was dealt with. He did so with both the clarity of someone who understood the need for swift action, and the compassion of someone who had seen his own family and friends have to fight, and flee, for their lives. It is safe to say that, with a different president, Kurdistan might not have been so safe, or so stable, during the conflict with ISIS. Nor would it have ridden out the economic and humanitarian troubles that followed quite so well.

In this, we can count Masoud Barzani as a success as a president, yet the moment that was almost his greatest success was also the moment that ultimately served to bring down his presidency and undo many of the gains that Kurdistan had made in the years under him. I am talking, of course, about the referendum of 2017.

CHAPTER TEN

Referendum

On the 25th September 2017, Kurdistan voted in the largest exercise of democracy it had ever experienced. More than three million people voted on the simple question of whether Kurdistan should become an independent state, separate from Iraq. More than 93% of those who voted did so in favour of separating from Iraq.

This part is a matter of public record, but how did Kurdistan get to this point. What made President Masoud Barzani decide that was the moment for a once in a lifetime vote? What made him decide on that instant, rather than another?

The general pressures towards independence have been detailed throughout this work. Over the course of his life, Masoud Barzani has been a proponent of Kurdish independence, even a symbol of it. He has fought against repressive governments that have sought to hold back that independence, and has consistently made the case for it as a leader and politician.

Throughout his time as Kurdistan's president, there was a sense that he wished eventually to bring about independence for Kurdistan. Even so, we must ask the question of how it came to happen in 2017. What elements came together to make it more feasible then that at some point in the past?

It wasn't a sudden upswing in public opinion calling for such a referendum. For as long as Kurdistan has existed, there appears to have been a substantial majority within it in favour of it being an independent state. Indeed, the ubiquity of and support for the independence movement in the decades when it was repressed, along with the many uprisings in favour of it, all suggest that there has long been a substantial majority in favour of independence. It wasn't public opinion that changed.

In relation to that, the referendum was originally discussed for 2014, but was shut down by political opposition, both within Kurdistan and in Iraq as the disputes between the Baghdad and Kurdistan governments rumbled on. The 2005 'referendum', which had no official status, also shows that this is an idea that has been around in Kurdistan for a long time, and is relatively well supported.

If it was not a shift in public opinion, nor was it that the government was finally one that was committed to such independence. By the time of the referendum, Masoud Barzani had been president for more than a decade, first of the version of Kurdistan that came into existence on the fall of Saddam, and then of the more formally constituted version. We have seen his commitment to independence throughout this work, so it isn't as if something changed for him there. Perhaps we could argue that the KDP was always held back in this regard by its political partners and opponents in Kurdistan, but even they have typically expressed support for independence in general terms, even if they have often tried to argue that a particular time was not right, or that Kurdistan's semi-autonomous status was enough for now. When the referendum did take place, the KDP was able to secure enough support to let it happen.

We are forced to conclude, therefore, that conditions must have shifted in some way that made it more possible to have the referendum, or even required it. There are several factors at play here.

One was the distraction of several of those who might have sought to stop such a referendum. In 2017, the war against ISIS was still ongoing, although perhaps not as intense as it had been. It meant that several of the nations that had sought to oppose Kurdish separatism in the past were now in a position where it seemed less likely that they could do so. Iraq, in particular, was caught up in the fight against ISIS, along with Turkey, Russia, Syria, and Iran. The result was the appearance of what seemed to be a clear field of play on which the referendum could take place, and it may have seemed to Masoud Barzani that an independent Kurdistan could be carved out in that moment, then settled into place so that no one could truly argue with it.

Economically, Kurdistan was coming out of a crash, which might not ordinarily seem like a reason for such a referendum, but the reasons for it may have added impetus. For months, Baghdad had not paid the money it was required to contribute to Kurdistan's budget under the Iraqi constitution. That failure effectively showed Kurdistan as a financially independent place, and created conditions of particular antipathy towards Baghdad that prepared the ground for the referendum to come.

One bright spot economically was that the conflict against ISIS had resulted in Kurdish control over the oil producing city of Kirkuk, formerly claimed by the Baghdad government, largely on the basis of Saddam's Arabization of it in the 1980s. ISIS had taken the city, and peshmerga forces had driven them out, giving the Kurdistan government clear control over a sustainable source of funds. Again, it pointed to the potential for Kurdistan to succeed as an independent nation.

There may also have been a measure of expectation on Masoud Barzani's part that this time there would be support from Kurdistan's international partners. Kurdistan had been at the forefront of the fight against ISIS, with the result that awareness of it and its desire for independence had risen among the public in a host of nations worldwide. There had been calls in the US for support for its independence, and there seemed to be a tacit understanding that Kurdistan was going to become independent in the wake of the war.

A part of this was the understanding that the region had already been destabilised by the war, and so it may have seemed obvious that this was the best moment in which to redraw the map of the Middle East in a way that included a new country. Iraq had already been broken apart by violence, so there were many commentators suggesting that it should be broken up more formally, with a three state solution touted as a possible option to resolve the existing conflicts within it.

All of these factors suggested that this might be a good moment in which to act, but there were also other factors that suggested that this might be the last chance for some time in which to do so.

One key one was that the fight against ISIS was slowly being won. Masoud Barzani would have known the history of his people, and his family. He would have known that traditionally, Kurdistan's allies have made many promises and half promises in times of war, only for those promises to melt away when peace has come. It is a process that occurred in the 1970s, 80s and 90s, and indeed even in the conflict that brought Iraq about: World War One. While Kurdish peshmerga had a key role to play in the fight, there was an opportunity to push for independence, but Masoud Barzani will have known that the moment that fight was won, its allies would have started to talk about the need for stability and the importance of not disrupting an already fragile region. As for its enemies, they would only stay distracted by the war for so long. Baghdad, in particular, was distracted by the war against ISIS in Iraq, so that it was not in a position to stop independence at first. However, as time wore on, it had greater resources to bring to bear in any attempt to bring Kurdistan back under control.

The notion of this being a last chance was relevant in demographic terms, too. Put simply, those individuals in Kurdistan who remember direct rule by Saddam's Iraq are getting older, while younger people don't understand the potential horrors that can come from being trapped as a part of Iraq in quite the same way. That is not to say that many young people aren't interested in independence, but to men of Masoud Barzani's generation, it may seem that they are shifting their attention to other issues, willing to accept a mere semi-autonomous status while concentrating more on elements such as economic prosperity or political structures. It may have seemed to Masoud Barzani that, if he did not secure an independence referendum then, at the peak of KDP support, there was a chance that other parties might have that support in future instead.

Finally, there was the issue of Masoud Barzani's presidency. Even prior to the referendum, it was obvious that it was growing close to the end. He had overrun the official term of the presidency because of the war, purely due to the emergency situation that it created. Some had already suggested that this meant he was trying to become a strongman president, an elected dictator trying to hollow out the democratic structures that he had played a role in constructing. It was obvious that, once the war against ISIS was settled, he would be faced with the choice of leaving office or openly moving towards dictatorship.

Because he knew that, and because of his commitment to moving Kurdistan towards being a more truly functioning democracy, Masoud Barzani must have felt that his opportunities to finally bring about independence were becoming more limited by the day. It had reached the point for him where, if he did not act, then he would be forced to stand back and watch, hoping that his successors would act instead. He would not be the man to complete things that had been started in Mahabad when he was born but, at best, a spectator to that completion. It seems impossible that he could have stood by, knowing that.

Instead, he did what he had been suggesting he would do for some time, and announced a referendum.

The referendum did not come out of nowhere. Kurdistan had already held a wide ranging opinion poll on the topic some years before, which some have erroneously called a referendum in the past, but which had neither the government backing nor sufficiently wide participation to truly provide a mandate for action. Equally, Masoud Barzani had made it clear for many years that he wished to move Kurdistan in the direction of full independence, and that he saw a referendum as a necessary way of securing a democratic mandate to do so. In this sense, the referendum cannot have come as a surprise to anyone.

It also came in a period where referenda had become briefly popular worldwide, with a greater focus on direct democracy seen as viable in an age where widespread access to information was seen as creating a more informed electorate in most countries. Other countries such as Switzerland had adopted low level referenda as a way of making any spending commitment, while there had been or soon would be referenda on issues such as Scottish independence and Brexit in the UK, and on Catalan independence just weeks before the Kurdish vote. Where previously, there had been the feeling that referenda were tools only for dictators to get the "will of the people" on their side to support their decisions, this came in a period where people felt that referenda could legitimately express popular will on specific questions better than representative politics.

In spite of this, opposition started to line up to the prospect of the referendum from the moment that Masoud Barzani announced it, and even before. Turkey, Iran and Syria all restated their opposition to such a move, and warned that they would close their borders, then seek to overturn the result. Baghdad stated quite clearly that it believed the referendum to have no validity, as it claimed that it ran counter to Iraq's constitution, and that only the Iraqi parliament would have the power to sanction such a thing.

There was international opposition prior to the referendum too, with several European countries talking about the disruption that it was likely to cause. The United States did not offer support either, because although Kurdistan was its ally, so was Iraq, and it felt that the referendum might trigger violence between the two that might then jeopardise the fight against ISIS. As on so many occasions previously, the US was prepared to offer kind words in the phase when it needed support from Kurdistan to reduce the number of American soldiers involved in a war, but was quick to withdraw it when Kurdistan began to seek independence in earnest.

There was another, more specific problem for the international community, which was that the referendum was just a little too late to catch the true wave of enthusiasm for such things internationally. In Europe, in particular, a series of difficult or unpopular referenda had created problems for governments, whether through the decision over Brexit and the narrow defeat of Scottish independence in the UK, or through the disputed referendum on Catalan independence. The latter, in particular, meant that Europe could never provide support to the Kurdish cause. If seen backing a referendum on independence held without the consent of the larger country that a region was claiming independence from, they would face accusations of hypocrisy over Catalonia and Spain's relationship.

Looking back, it is easy to see that this fit the pattern of multiple earlier events, where Kurdistan attempted to push towards independence, expecting international support, only to see it evaporating as the possibility grew closer. Why then did Masoud Barzani continue, when he must have been able to read the signs?

It seems here that there has been a calculation involved in Kurdistan's attempts at independence, which is that, if Kurdistan can only get it done, and can maintain it even a little while, then it is likely to be able to continue. The notion is that if Kurdistan can set itself up as an independent nation, then the international order is likely to opt for stability rather than for the upheaval of its removal. This is a view, though, that may underestimate the sheer hatred of some of Kurdistan's neighbours for any prospect of its independence. It may also overestimate the willingness of the international community to act in the area.

There was probably another consideration for Masoud Barzani, which is that historically, even the moments when Kurdistan's pushes for independence have failed have helped to keep the dream of it alive. In the coverage these moments have gathered, and in the memories of pain that they have built, they have helped to build momentum for the next push, serving the narrative of the small nation held down by 25th its larger neighbours.

There is also a sense in which Masoud Barzani was trapped by the narrative that he and others had constructed around him for so long. He was the leader who pushed consistently towards independence, and so there was no reasonable way in which he could turn down the prospect of moving towards it now that he had set himself on that course. Having announced the referendum, he could not back away from it, even though there were some signs that he was all too aware of the dangers that it potentially posed. After all, he announced that the result might not be put into practice straight away, clearly trying to avoid the worst conflicts that such a move might cause.

Because he was so bound up with the narrative of independence, and because he believed in it, the only move was to go ahead and call the referendum. The process of calling it was anything but simple, though. President Barzani built up to the announcement of a referendum several times in the months before, only for the ongoing campaign against ISIS to disrupt the possibility of it, with the need to maintain some level of cooperation with Baghdad's forces seen as important in maintaining pressure against an enemy that would otherwise represent a threat to Kurdistan as an entity.

Even so, it gradually became clear that 2017 would be the year in which the referendum would take place, and on the 7th of June 2017, President Barzani called a meeting between the various political parties of Kurdistan, after which he announced that the referendum would take place on the 25th September 2017. From that moment, two clocks were ticking simultaneously: one organisational, and the other a countdown to whatever reaction would come from around Kurdistan.

The organisational clock is surprisingly interesting, because it is easy to forget the sheer scale of human endeavour involved in a process such as this. Elections take place in stable, democratic countries on a relatively regular schedule, yet even in those countries a snap election or a nationwide vote can catch people by surprise, forcing sleepless nights for those civil servants tasked with delivering the election day. A referendum adds another layer of complexity, because it is not the old, familiar electoral system known to everyone, but a one off question where every vote must be counted across the region where it is held. A question must be framed carefully, so as to avoid prejudicing the answers people give, counters must be trained, and lines of communication must be put in place to ensure that not one vote is missed. We know, as a point of comparison for a region with a broadly similar size of population, that the Scottish Independence vote of 2014 had a final administrative cost of more than £15million.

That is difficult and expensive enough, but now imagine doing it in a region experiencing ongoing conflict, without the support of the central government claiming overall constitutional control of Iraq. Already, ordinary elections had found themselves disrupted by the violence of the fight against ISIS, while the poll had been put back several times in order to allow it to fit in with the needs of the conflict. Elections in all areas of Iraq have long been targets for violence, with the need for the police or military protection of polling centres to be balanced against the potential for such an armed presence to disrupt the fairness of the polling. The scale of the security operation for the referendum was substantial, especially given the number of state and non-state actors who had previously expressed their opposition.

In the run up to the referendum, those opposed included all of the countries surrounding Kurdistan, several European countries, and the United States. There were a number of neutral parties, such as Jordan, but very few that were actively pro-referendum. Of them, Israel was the only recognised state, taking its position based on the perception of a shared status as a homeland for a people, whose very right to exist has been attacked by an otherwise dominant Arab majority in the region. Other support came from factions within governments, individual parties, and particularly separatist groups elsewhere. There was support, for example, from Quebec and Catalonia, both of which have strong elements seeking to break away from the larger countries that contain them. As welcome as this support was, in some respects it was less than helpful, as it reduced support from elsewhere. Israel's support meant that none of its enemies would ever support the referendum (although, to be fair, many of them would never have done so anyway). The support of other independence movements meant that governments were reminded that giving support to Kurdistan would have been a tacit approval of moves by their own groups to declare independence.

It is in this phase that Masoud Barzani somewhat lost control of the story being told around the world about Kurdistan. In the previous few years, it had been a story of plucky Kurdish peshmerga, fighting against the west's enemies for it, and contributing to the stability of a region that most western powers wanted to pull out of when it was feasible to do so in order to bring an end to what seemed like endless fighting in the wake of the invasion of Iraq.

Instead, the story became the one that Baghdad told: of a region risking further disruption and conflict by insisting on something that none of its neighbours wanted, holding an 'illegal' and 'unconstitutional' referendum to do so. Even among most areas that were well disposed towards Kurdistan, that claim of the illegality of the referendum seemed to find some purchase. The Dutch consul general to Kurdistan, for example, argued that the referendum would have far more support worldwide if it were seen as taking place in consultation with Baghdad.

Parts of the story were based on false information. Television and social media outlets outside Kurdistan seemed to be happy, in the run up to the referendum, to circulate false stories, alleging that a yes vote would result in an influx of Jewish settlers, or uprisings in the surrounding regions, or the destruction of the economy. In the absence of any penalties for these untruths, even retractions wouldn't have made a difference, because by then, the ideas were in people's heads.

Ultimately though, it didn't make much of a difference. The referendum went ahead in the face of that, and it was successful, which is to say that it took place with only minor violence and disruption. Officials were able to conduct polling and prevent electoral fraud, with the result that the referendum went ahead as planned. In the run up to the referendum, polling suggested figures of about 55 percent in favour, 25 percent against, and 30 percent undecided.

In the event, the actual poll results went beyond anything anyone could have hoped, with more than 93 percent of those who voted doing so in favour of independence. This is such a huge figure that it might seem at first glance like the kind of referendum found throughout history where dictators have used plebiscites to have almost total 'support' for their actions.

Yet, as far as we can tell, this was a fair referendum. As such, how can we explain this, especially given the apparent commitment of so many in opinion polls to vote against?

Partly, this can be explained by the nature of opinion polls, which, depending on the methods employed and the sample, can occasionally be wide of the mark. In a situation where regular polling with a representative sample might have been difficult, it is possible that the opinion poll mentioned may simply not have been correct.

It is also possible that opinions may have changed in the time since that poll. It is possible that the hostility from regions outside Kurdistan may have backfired, reminding people of the days when they were alone against the world and driving them together. It is possible that, in treating Kurdistan as something to be ordered around, they created the conditions for people to push back, voting yes.

Equally, it is possible that potential no voters stayed away from the referendum. It is a common thing in referenda where one side seems to have a clear lead. Those who are opposed sometimes respond either with apathy, wondering what the point is of showing up to vote, or with a deliberate disengagement from the process; knowing that the lower the turnout is, the less legitimacy can be attached to a vote. In Catalonia, for example, much of the anti-independence side deliberately didn't vote, because they wanted to make it clear that in their eyes it was an illegitimate poll.

Whatever the reasons, the result of the independence referendum was utterly one sided. It was clear that the people of Kurdistan wanted it to be an independent nation, and Masoud

Barzani appeared to have achieved, not just his lifetime's dream, but that of his father and grandfather as well.

So, what happened next?

Aftermath

The referendum was not designed to be immediately binding, in the sense that it would not trigger an immediate declaration of independence. Instead, the weight of the referendum result was meant to be a bargaining chip in negotiations with the Baghdad government, designed to lead to the eventual result of a completely independent country.

Part of the reason for emphasising this was to contain some of the celebrations that sprang up in the wake of the referendum result. These celebrations contained some measure of rioting and disruption, and also served to trigger parallel demonstrations in regions outside of Iraqi Kurdistan. These demonstrations may have contributed to some of the trouble that followed, because they mainly took place in Kurdish areas of surrounding countries, such as Iran. In Iran, there were several arrests for singing the anthem of the Republic of Mahabad, and for illegal assembly, as people there started to demand independence along with Iraqi Kurdistan.

That triggered the worst fears of the surrounding regimes, confirming to them that the push for independence in Iraqi Kurdistan would only lead to their own Kurdish populations seeking similar levels of autonomy. This meant that instantly, Kurdistan found itself cut off, with surrounding countries starting to close their borders, perhaps to prevent any exodus of their citizens into the region.

The results of this were anything but the independent state that Masoud Barzani was seeking to achieve. If anything, the aftermath of the referendum pushed Kurdistan further from that independence, taking away control of key resources and damaging its capacity to defend itself against further aggression. It also did harm to some of the international support that it believed it had, exposing the true situation for Kurdistan while also squandering whatever power had come from at least the appearance of international aid.

Rioting

One issue with the referendum's aftermath was that so little of it was controllable. While Masoud Barzani was the region's president, there were large populations of Kurds, and large areas, that fell outside of his control. The reactions of some of those areas presented problems for the process of the referendum, and for the possibility of a negotiated Kurdistan independence.

In Iran, in the largely Kurdish cities of Baneh, Sanandaj and Mahabad, the reaction was sudden, joyous, but also dangerous. There are reports of people singing the former national anthem of the Mahabad Republic in the referendum's wake, and certainly of large scale gatherings in the streets, some of which were described as celebrations, some of which were described as demonstrations demanding their own independence, or even as riots by the authorities.

Certainly, in the immediate aftermath of the referendum result, it seems to have been impossible for the wider Kurdish world to contain its reaction to what seemed to have been the realisation of the dream of independence. Indeed, how could anyone have expected them to contain that response? It was both predictable, and predicted, that a vote for independence would spark similar demands in neighbouring areas, along with some degree of celebration, unrest, and public disruption. Kurdistan's neighbours had based some of their warnings about the referendum on precisely the threat of such disruption, with Iran and Turkey both expressing concerns about the possibility of a domino effect when they have historically had ongoing conflicts with Kurdish separatist groups in their own border areas.

The immediate result of these demonstrations/celebrations was mass arrests. It is hard to know exactly how many people were arrested, since Iran's security apparatus is not in the business of releasing such details to the outside world, but we do know that the arrests moved beyond the usual targeted snatching of key dissidents, into the blanket detention of anyone who was in the area. The idea from their side was to sap momentum from any move towards uprising on their side of the border, yet in truth, it was never likely to happen. Masoud Barzani's government had specifically been seeking to avoid that kind of response, to try to avoid creating the feeling of disturbance in the region. Instead, it had been trying to sell the world the idea that it was simply normalising the status quo.

What were the effects of these demonstrations? Perhaps what those involved hoped was that they would be the start of a wider uprising, that would create a kind of Greater Kurdistan that would take in the areas of Syria that were Kurdish held as a result of the conflict with ISIS there, the parts of Iran that were closest to Iraq, and the areas of Turkey that had long been subjected to conflict with its own separatist movements.

The actual effect was to provide evidence to both Kurdistan's neighbours and the wider world that this danger was a reality. By emphasising the disruptive nature of the demonstrations, Iran and other neighbours had a justification for their ensuing aggression towards Kurdistan, for the military build ups, the sanctions, and the border closures. By emphasising this disruption, meanwhile, Kurdistan's neighbours were able to create a story for the wider world of an even that was going to destabilise a situation in and around Iraq that was only just starting to come under control.

The reason for mentioning this is to show the role of events outside of Masoud Barzani's control in this period. There is a temptation in the biographies of leaders to suggest that everything that happened was down to their actions or inactions. In this case, it is tempting, because the referendum was Masoud Barzani's project, to see all that follows as flowing from that decision. At the same time though, we must remember the role that elements like this played, with the reaction of broad swathes of the wider Kurdish population having an effect that Masoud Barzani could not control, even if he might have been able to predict it.

Ultimately, the demonstrations themselves were not as important as the stories told about them. This was something that Masoud Barzani would have understood, since his whole life had been shaped by the expectations and stories told around him. In letting Kurdistan's neighbours control the shape of the story being told about the referendum, the region let the aftermath get out of its control, and paved the way for the breakdown of international relations that followed.

Preparations for Independence

There was a brief delay following the referendum, in which it was made clear by Masoud Barzani that independence would not be declared immediately, but instead worked towards with the involvement of all stakeholders within the region. Crucially, this meant talks with both Baghdad and with other parties within Kurdistan.

That is why Masoud Barzani requested talks with Baghdad, seeking a way to move to independence in a peaceful manner. Perhaps he thought that with the weight of the referendum behind him, he would now be in a good bargaining position, or perhaps he felt that it was a necessary step in order to gain international support. Either way, it failed, because Baghdad refused to even discuss the possibility, moving immediately to military action.

Masoud Barzani also sought to create a political leadership body to prepare the way for independence, based on cross party talks to establish how it should work. The body was intended to show that independence was a project for the whole of Kurdistan, not just the KDP. Perhaps if it had been taken in those terms by the others who had the potential to be involved, they might have chosen to play a part.

Instead, they stayed away. Part of the reason for this is that they saw the body as an attempt by Masoud Barzani to assert control over the emerging country. Perhaps a more relevant reason was that they started to see the backlash coming, and chose to make sure that independence remained associated with Masoud Barzani, rather than them. As such, the other parties of Kurdistan refused to join the political leadership body, and it failed.

International Relations

The immediate aftermath of the referendum was catastrophic in terms of Kurdistan's international relations. President Barzani had been banking on the idea that, by acting in a way that was fundamentally democratic, by demonstrating the clear will of the Kurdish people, and by seeking dialogue with Baghdad rather than declaring independence outright, he would be able to maintain the support of Kurdistan's European and North American partners, who would then put pressure on its neighbours to minimise any backlash from the likes of Iran or Turkey. He may even have believed that, while those neighbours would make further noises about the repercussions of independence, they would not actually act. Indeed, there are some suggestions that his contacts with the leaders of Kurdistan's neighbours had given him exactly that impression.

In this, President Barzani was mistaken. There is no other way to put it, but it is an understandable mistake, since it is, in many ways, the same misjudgement that has come up in the policies of Kurdistan since the 1920s. There has been a tendency for hope to triumph over experience, with successive generations of Kurdish politicians, fighters and rebels willing to believe that *this* time, the international community would live up to its vague promises regarding Kurdistan.

President Masoud Barzani believed that the reaction from Kurdistan's neighbours would be manageable, because he wanted to believe it. He believed that America might support a move towards independence in spite of the many occasions in the past when it has abandoned Kurdistan on the cusp of it, because he wanted it to be true. In this, we must remember that the holder of the president's office is ultimately a man and not some perfect figure. The very desire to push towards independence that had fuelled so much of Masoud Barzani's life let him down here.

Would anyone else have seen things otherwise? Clearly there are some others who warned of it, but almost by definition, anyone who had worked towards independence for any length of time would have responded in the same ways. It seems unreasonable to expect that anyone who had managed to get into the position Masoud Barzani found himself in would have acted otherwise.

Yet the impacts on Kurdistan's international relations were real, and must be detailed.

The immediate impacts on its relations with its neighbours involved the breakdown of the unsteady fragments of peace that had been built up. Several neighbours immediately closed their borders, partly to prevent the possibility of any mass exodus of their Kurdish populations, and partly to limit the possibility of any conflict spilling over their borders. It is something that these countries had done before, but now it had another impact: it was effectively a trade embargo, cutting off Kurdistan from any of its means of making money in the world. Kurdistan's reliance on oil meant that such an embargo limited its resources, while also preventing it from bringing in food and medicine from the outside. It did not amount to a direct attack, but it was as good as sanctioning one.

The attitude from outside was largely one of condemnation or deliberate ignorance, in line with countries' earlier positions. Europe stood largely neutral on the issue, expressing worries that it their earlier concerns about the destabilisation of the region were true. They sent no aid, although they did express the desire that the matter should be resolved peacefully. Again, it was a sign to Baghdad that there would be no real reprisals if they took action.

The USA's reaction was exactly what Kurdistan should have expected: it did nothing. Again, that was almost the same thing as sanctioning what was to follow.

There was some hope that perhaps Baghdad might be willing to talk. Masoud Barzani expressed that hope himself when he suggested that the result of the referendum would not be implemented immediately, and that he would seek to begin talks with Iraq's federal government. Of course, we know that the invasion that followed was the reply, and that Baghdad was not even willing to discuss the implications of the referendum in the longer term.

The longer term impacts of the referendum on international relations are hard to pin down precisely. It seems to have produced some antipathy towards Iran's increased involvement in Kurdish affairs within Kurdistan, as a result of Iran's role within the aftermath. It has increased the sense that Baghdad will never accept a peaceful solution to the idea of Kurdish independence, and that may have increased the likelihood of violent action to bring it about in the future. It has reinforced the sense that, no matter what the local conditions, no matter how it might seem that it might benefit them to support independence, Kurdistan fundamentally cannot trust its neighbours to do anything but stand against it.

As for the wider world, the old adage has been shown to be true: Kurdistan has no friends but the mountains. The failure of European and American partners to provide support in the moment that mattered most showed that those relationships are essentially one sided, with America in particular only interested in using Kurdistan as a proxy in the region not tied to its opponents.

Perhaps in time, Kurdistan will learn that lesson. Frequently in Masoud Barzani's life, circumstances have shown that those who create the illusion of being willing to help do not truly have any desire to do so. Perhaps the biggest long term impact of the referendum on Kurdistan's international relations will be that it will come to understand that fact. Perhaps in the longer term, it will be less willing to act as a proxy for outside forces, but also less willing to pin its hopes on help that doesn't come.

Perhaps if it does so, it will never find itself in the situation again where it stands waiting, while Baghdad advances upon it.

Territorial Losses

The military action by Baghdad was relatively short. Even prior to the referendum, its troops had been blockading routes into Mosul and Dohuk, seeking to cut off free movement into and out of the region. It made demands that Kurdistan should hand over control of its airports, and when it refused, banned flights to and from them. Coupled with the actions of Kurdistan's neighbours, the result was a progressive isolation of the region, in a way that may have been designed to get it to back down, but which has typically been seen as a build up to conflict.

The threats continued to build, as Iraq held what it termed 'joint exercises' with the Iranians, on Iran's border with Kurdistan. That allowed for a build up of tanks and armoured vehicles there, as well as preventing any crossing over the border. It also made demands regarding Kurdistan ceding territories that it had secured during the conflict with ISIS, but which it felt were Iraqi, regarding the control of the airports, and about the transfer of funds to Baghdad over oil issues. To those who had lived through other attacks by Iraq, the signs must have been ominous.

At this stage, we must ask a couple of questions. First, what kind of Iraqi government would make those kinds of threats against a region that had already suffered genocide in its history? What does it take to evoke the memory of such events, and other violent repressions, in an attempt to get your opponents to back down?

It is relatively easy to understand the mindset of the Iraq government in general: they saw Kurdistan as *theirs*, and it didn't matter what its people thought about it. It is a way of thinking that is common in larger countries with smaller separatist regions. 'We decide whether you should have a referendum,' they declare, or even, 'why shouldn't the population of the whole (larger) country have a say in whether you are a part of it?' It is a reaction that has been found around the world, everywhere from Spain's reaction to the Catalan independence referendum, to Scottish calls for a second independence referendum, to colonies held by larger powers. It is a kind of 'finders keepers' attitude, in which, because they or their ancestors happened to take or be given control of a place, they feel that things should always be that way. In some senses, one of the key elements of calling for independence is to expose this, and to show that claims over regions typically do not rest on any kind of democratic mandate, but on military force.

The second question we must ask is why Masoud Barzani, and Kurdistan in general, did not back down at this stage. Part of the answer to that is that the referendum's result compelled him not to. How could he say that he didn't want independence when he had all his life, and when more than nine tenths of Kurdistan's voters supported the idea? Perhaps part of the answer is that he felt that, if he refused to back down, he would compel the other side to talk. Maybe he hoped that the threat of a conflict would force international partners to step in and broker peace talks that would then bring about a peaceful transition to independence. He had already stated earlier in the year that he had talked with the Iraqi prime minister, and that he had agreed with Masoud Barzani's desire to have peaceful talks in the wake of any referendum. Perhaps it is even possible that he believed that this posturing was a necessary face saving exercise for Iraq, which would then give way to pragmatism and the promised phase of discussions.

If so, it was not to be. Two weeks after the start of the exercises, perhaps when it became clear that Kurdistan was not about to give in to Baghdad's demands, Iraqi forces advanced on the city of Kirkuk, which has long been a disputed area between Kurdistan and Baghdad. The heart of its importance is its oil resources, which is why ISIS sought to capture it from Iraqi control during its rise, and why Kurdish peshmerga fought hard to take it back. It is a city that was originally predominantly Kurdish, but was then subjected to extensive Arabisation under Saddam, and which is vital to the economies of both areas. It was almost inevitable that the violence would start there.

Baghdad's army rolled in, and encountered little resistance, since the peshmerga stationed in Kirkuk were ordered to withdraw by their commanders. There have been many arguments over the reasoning behind this. There have been those who have tried to portray the commanders as traitors to Kurdistan, or as supporting the idea of Kurdistan within Iraq. Others have suggested that they saw the overwhelming nature of Iraq's heavy armour, and wanted to avoid a pointless slaughter. Perhaps it is even possible that, remembering the way peshmerga had traditionally conducted war, they sought to melt away now so that there might be a chance to come back and strike later.

Whatever the reason, resistance to the Iraqi invasion fell apart both suddenly and utterly. Iraqi forces were able to recapture almost all of the territories that Kurdistan had expanded into over the decades since the initial settlement of the region's borders, reclaiming areas that it had so spectacularly failed to defend from ISIS when it came to seize them previously.

Over just ten days, years of work was undone. By the time the ceasefire came on the 25th of October, Kurdistan was in as bad a state as it had been in since before the fall of Saddam. The push towards independence had done the opposite, and led to Iraqi tanks on its soil, while around Iraq, there were attacks on Kurds living outside Kurdistan's borders.

Resignation

President Masoud Barzani offered his resignation on the 28th of October 2017, to become effective on the 1st of November. We must ask what prompted him to resign then, what it must have felt like for him in that moment, what it meant for Kurdistan and the KDP, and what it meant for Kurdish independence.

What must it have been like for him in that moment? Kurdistan's independence was a cause that Masoud Barzani had worked towards from a young age, that he had been entwined with since the moment that he was born. It had seemed, for one brief moment, for just a matter of days, that it might be something that would finally come to fruition. Then it was taken away from him, suddenly and utterly, with the gains that had been made under his presidency largely wiped away. The project that he had put so much into was gone, and now he had to resign as well. It is hard to express how difficult that act of resignation must have been for him.

Why resign? In part, it was *because* a project that was so bound up with him had been torn apart so completely. It was a necessary symbol to those attacking Kurdistan that, for now at least, it had backed down. It was a necessary response to a situation where Masoud Barzani was so caught up with the attempt at independence that, had he remained, it would have seemed like an attempt to continue it. It is even seen as normal in many places that, when a politician is intimately bound up with a project, and that project does not go to plan, they resign in order to allow the rest of the political process to move forward.

In another sense, the referendum was always going to be a kind of final act as president. Even had the referendum succeeded, it is possible that he might have stepped back. The referendum's timing was, as we have seen, at least partly because Masoud Barzani knew that his time as president was limited (indeed, that only the emergency situation of the war with ISIS had kept his presidency going as long as it had). In a sense, independence via the referendum was intended as the crowning achievement of his career. Resignation thus became the natural finish to events. This was not the time for him to start again.

It was, however, the moment for a new generation to take over. For some years prior to his resignation, Masoud Barzani's younger family members had been filling increasing responsible roles within both the KDP and the government. It is possible that he saw that moment as an opportunity for new figures to step into place, with that being seen as a natural, positive thing.

There is also a sense in which resignation was the natural course because Masoud Barzani had come to see the limits of the political process in making Kurdistan independent. He had spent years testing the idea that Kurdistan could become independent through political means: by building international relationships, by demonstrating public support for the idea, and by being a good regional partner demonstrating that it was no threat to the surrounding countries. He had tested the idea that some amount of advancement of Kurdistan in the political, economic or social sphere would be enough to give it independence. The moments after the referendum demonstrated that it was not going to be enough, that Kurdistan's political system could ultimately only affect Kurdistan. Faced with that, was there any *point* in still being president.

There is, of course, an extent to which the resignation was forced by outside pressure. Because Masoud Barzani was very much the symbol of the independence movement, it seems unlikely that Kurdistan's opponents would ever have backed down had he not resigned. It was a necessary component of the cessation of hostilities. In that sense, his resignation was what most of the other acts of Masoud Barzani's life had been: an attempt to do what was best for Kurdistan.

Relations with Baghdad

The lasting effects on relations with Baghdad of the referendum have yet to be fully seen. However, there were sudden, and substantial, effects that must be discussed. The first of these was the immediate "freezing" of the referendum's result, stalling the movement towards independence. There were discussions, but not the discussions on moving towards independence that Masoud Barzani had intended. Instead, they were discussions of the nature of the ongoing relationship between the two, and Kurdistan had relatively little say in it.

Iraq's supreme court made the definitive declaration regarding this, stating that it was illegal, and unconstitutional, for any part of Iraq to attempt to secede from it. It was a clear statement that Iraq never intended to let Kurdistan go. There were then further talks about the kind of relationship that

Kurdistan and Iraq will have, but ultimately, that is not something that can be decided in such an environment. It is about human reactions to one another.

It is likely that an antagonistic note has been confirmed for the future between Kurdistan and Iraq. Iraq has confirmed that it will always consider Kurdistan as belonging to it, and Kurdistan's referendum confirmed the strength of its desire to be independent. This moment has shown that there will continue to be flash points between the two.

There is likely to be a repositioning of the economic relationship between the two, especially with the recapturing of Kirkuk. Given the instability and tensions of much of Iraq, Kurdistan still remains the most stable part of it, but it now lacks the economic independence given to it by its oil resources in quite the same way it had before. That makes the process of any future divergence a little more complex than it was.

There is likely to be even more mistrust in future than there was before between Baghdad and Kurdistan. While there was never likely to be immediate friendship between the two, there had been a generation growing up in Kurdistan that had never known an attack by Iraqi forces. That seemed to be the most likely route to rapprochement between the two. Now though, another generation has seen the willingness of the Iraqi state to use force to prevent Kurdistan becoming an entity in its own right.

There are likely to be discussions about their political interactions too. If Kurdistan feels that it cannot believe anything Baghdad says, and Baghdad sees Kurdistan as a rebellious force needing to be suppressed, how can the two seriously engage with one another in order to produce beneficial outcomes for their citizens?

One complicating factor in this seems to be a new strategy that Masoud Barzani is adopting: one of seeking to increase Kurdish influence within Baghdad. While Jalal Talabani had a period as Iraqi president, that was of limited overall benefit to Kurdistan. What *might* work is the election of Kurdish officials to as many roles as possible within Iraq. While it might look like some kind of acceptance of the current relationship between Baghdad and Kurdistan, it actually serves to create the conditions for a peaceful, mutually agreed independence at some point in the future. It represents an understanding on Masoud Barzani's part that Iraq's constitution and the unwillingness of the outside world to go against that make it difficult if not impossible to achieve independence without some control within Baghdad.

In times like these, there are instabilities that make government as normal difficult. Standard lines of communication will have a role to play, but there will also be a need for other ways of doing things, and other figures to play a role. Perhaps, just perhaps, this future relationship between Kurdistan and Baghdad has a role for figures such as the now former president?

Current Role

Masoud Barzani's current role is ambiguous. Since his resignation, he has stepped back from the formal politics of the Kurdistan region, meaning that he plays no part in or around Kurdistan's parliament, he is not the one to formally meet visiting dignitaries, and he does not have the final legal say on those of Kurdistan's decision making processes decided by the president.

In this sense, he is no longer the public figure that he was, and perhaps a reader from outside the Middle East might be forgiven for thinking that he is happily retired somewhere, living out his days quietly, with limited continuing influence on the region. Yes, he pops up on the news to comment on events, but that is the norm in most mature democracies, where a former president will often still at least have a voice that the media will amplify, even if they often have no formal power. In the United States, for example, a number of former presidents can occasionally be found commenting on public affairs, especially in the era of social media, while even more have charitable concerns.

In that sense, an outside observer might think of Masoud Barzani's current situation as being something along the same lines, yet in certain crucial respects, his current situation is different. For one thing, although he has stepped back from the presidency of Kurdistan, Masoud Barzani remains the head of the KDP, with substantial powers within its structures and a significant say regarding the formation of the party's policies. He remains in at least titular control of peshmerga forces as well, and, while outside visitors certainly come to see the new president, Nechirvan Barzani, they also make a point of speaking with Masoud Barzani where they can. This is not just a matter of ceremony, either, in the way that a foreign dignitary visiting England might have an audience with the queen before moving on to the real business of government with ministers and official. Masoud Barzani retains significant real power within Kurdistan, even in the wake of his resignation.

Obviously, to those unfamiliar with Kurdistan, or with the Middle East more generally, this situation might look somewhat alarming. It might look like someone attempting to be a de facto ruler, ignoring the democratic process and clinging to power with a kind of veneer of democracy in front of him. This is not in fact the case, though.

Firstly, we must remember that in the Middle East generally, and in a number of other regions in the world, it is entirely normal to have a head of a political party who is not the president of a region run by that party. It is common for numerous presidents and prime ministers to come from within the ranks of a party, while a respected elder statesman figure continues to have a significant say in the running of the party as a whole. It is a case where differences in norms can create the illusion of something wrong occurring.

Secondly, we must remember that the parallel power of Kurdistan's major political parties is not part of some plot for the future, but is instead a relic of past days. Masoud Barzani and others have seen throughout his life how easily the political structures of Kurdistan can be pulled apart by violence from outside. The urge to maintain what is often effectively a shadow government does not come from any desire to run a dictatorship, but is instead intended as a bulwark against the collapse of existing structures. In the continuing chaotic times for Kurdistan, caught between Baghdad and the hope for independence, it is a necessary element. It seems likely, however, that such structures would fade into those of the Kurdish state were Kurdistan to become truly independent.

Thirdly, we must remember that this role is subject to some level of democratic checks and balances, as the leadership of the KDP is an elected role within the party. We do not know yet if Masoud Barzani will at some point step back from his current position, or even if someone else from within the party will step up to take that position, yet it is a long way from being the untouchable point of control it might first appear to be.

One of the key elements of Masoud Barzani's current position is that it is founded on a level of respect for him as a statesman and a leader. There have been calls outside Kurdistan, even in the south of Iraq, for him to mediate in other disputes, and for him to play a role as a potential leader in other environments that are lacking one.

In this sense, it is likely that, even if he does end up with no formal position in Kurdistan's politics, he will still be a voice that is listened to, and will still be able to provide advice to the generations that have followed him. This is especially likely since his family is almost certain to continue to play a role in Kurdistan's governmental structures.

It seems likely that Masoud Barzani's role will continue to develop from his current position. It will be interesting to see if at some point, he does feel in a position to embrace a fuller kind of retirement from politics, leading the way for a transformation in the way that politics is done, not just within Kurdistan, but within the wider Middle East. Such a situation is likely only to happen in the event of an independent Kurdistan, however. For the moment, it is more likely that he will remain at the head of a secondary structure of governance until such time as he feels confident in handing it over to his sons and nephews.

Lessons for Future

Are there lessons for the future to be drawn from Masoud Barzani's handling of the referendum, and from events in its aftermath? Just as there are lessons to be drawn from so much else of his life, there are certainly things to learn from this chapter.

Most of the lessons are persistent ones in Kurdistan's history. There is the gap between what Kurdistan's allies say and what they will do. There is the risk of overestimating the security of Kurdistan's position. There is the delicate balance between the need for disruption to allow Kurdistan to break free, and the fears that others will have regarding that disruption. There is the distance between what the people of Kurdistan want, and what the situation around it will allow. And then there is the political difficulty, where the drive towards independence creates popularity, but also forces leaders to take actions that they know might be a risk.

The first of these elements, the gap between promises and actions among Kurdistan's allies, is almost as old as the history of revolt in the region. Whether it is the Soviets withdrawing support to Mahabad, the Americans brokering Iran-Iraq peace in the 1980s while forgetting the Kurds, or the most recent general noises of support for Kurdistan while allowing Baghdad to send in tanks, the truth is that Kurdistan's allies mostly think about what they can get from Kurdistan as a proxy in the region. They ally with Kurdistan for what they can get from it, not what they can give to it. They certainly see no reason to risk conflict in order to prop it up as an independent state. Masoud Barzani has seen examples of this throughout his life, yet the referendum also shows how circumstances on the ground can override such knowledge.

The risk of overestimating Kurdistan's position is another lesson. Several times now, Kurdistan has gotten to positions where it has felt that independence has been viable. It has felt its military forces to be powerful, its territory secure, and yet, outside armies have been able to overrun its positions. In the case of the recent referendum, the temptation was to see the war against ISIS as distracting the countries around Kurdistan to the extent that they could not, or would not, act against it. It was a necessary calculation, but it was also a mistake, as it proved that Baghdad was able to send heavy armour north, calculating that the preservation of its oil supplies was worth the risk.

Understanding where power lies in the wider political system is also vital. Kurdistan wishes to be free from Baghdad precisely because it holds too much power over it, and is willing to misuse that power. That, means, though, that Baghdad has the power to hang on to Kurdistan against its will. It demonstrated this in the days after the referendum, when it seemed that Kurdistan had its best chance at independence, but Baghdad had the military, diplomatic and political power to prevent that independence. Kurdistan found out the hard way that it is not enough for a decision about its future to be made in Kurdistan; it must be made in Baghdad, too.

So, what can Masoud Barzani do in the future to overcome those challenges? Part of it is greater engagement with the Baghdad system, making sure that as many Kurdish politicians as possible end up in positions of authority within the wider Iraqi system, because that is the only way to influence things in the direction of independence. If Iraqi politicians will not deal respectfully or honestly with Kurdistan, then it is important to ensure that Kurdish politicians are in the positions to make those decisions. As important as the Kurdistan Regional Government is to Kurdistan, it is vital for Masoud Barzani to recognise that it is not where many key decisions affecting Kurdistan are likely to be made.

That is preparation for the political aspect of it. There needs to be diplomatic preparation, but we need to consider exactly how much is possible in that regard. Masoud Barzani already engaged in considerable diplomatic efforts around the world to try to get Kurdistan's partners to to the point where they are prepared to support its independence, yet when the moment came, they stood back with vague condemnation. Unless Masoud Barzani is able to move Kurdistan's relations with the outside world beyond one where Kurdistan is merely looking after other countries' interests in the region, Kurdistan will never have a relationship that is more than one way, and will never be able to count on support from outside.

In this, picking the moment remains crucial. It is understandable that Kurdistan wishes to pick a moment of disruption in which to take its independence, yet there is a danger in this that such independence becomes only temporary. The very disruption creates a desire by the outside world to see things settled and stable, which means that it will typically stand back while Kurdistan's neighbours destroy that independence.

The third aspect is military preparation. Kurdistan has already gained some arms and equipment, training and other support as a result of the fight against ISIS, but it remains militarily less powerful than Baghdad, at least in terms of holding territory. The peshmerga will always be skilled in guerrilla war, but that is not what is needed to hold onto an emerging state. Perhaps Kurdistan can look to the example of Israel in this, which has been able to hold territory in spite of relatively small state, based on technological superiority and a high level of involvement of ordinary people in the military. How can such technological superiority be achieved, though, when the outside world is unlikely to treat Kurdistan in a separate way to Baghdad? Again, the answers come back to levels of political and diplomatic engagement.

It is vital that Masoud Barzani, and Kurdistan more generally, learn the lessons of the past. They must find a way to break free of the pattern of rebellion and crackdown that has plagued Kurdistan's past. Doing that will involve more than just waiting for a moment, or looking inward. It will need a level of engagement, not just with the outside world, but also with the very system that it is seeking to pull away from.

CHAPTER ELEVEN

Conclusion

HOW DO WE sum up a life, when it has had so many phases? More than that, how do we do so when there may be phases still to come. The historian Herodotus tells us that we should count no man as happy until his end is known, because there are too many ways for a life to twist and turn when its story is still unfinished.

Masoud Barzani's life has had more acts than most. He has been watched and mistrusted as a child. He has been a fighter. He has been a leader. He has fought for his country and fought to protect people who would otherwise be slaughtered. He has helped to build one country and nearly broken free of it. He has seen the largest outpouring of democratic will in modern times, and he has had to watch as that decision was overturned from military pressure from outside Kurdistan. He has helped Western allies bring an end to the fight against ISIS in Iraq, and at the same time worked to produce a fairer society within Kurdistan.

He has not been perfect, but that is a curiously modern requirement for our leaders. Because more people have access to more information than at any time in the past, we are more likely to know about the foibles, mistakes, and impossible decisions that mar the records of otherwise great people. We must remember that those in the past had just as many flaws, and made just as many difficult decisions, if not more. Yes, it is right that we should hold those elements up to the light of scrutiny, but it is also vital that we do not permit this to obscure the good that they have done.

In many ways, the pattern of Masoud Barzani's life is entirely consistent with what we would expect for leaders in newly emerging countries (as Kurdistan is in all but name). He is a man who has had to make the difficult transition from war leader to democratic president, moving from a situation where highly centralised, high speed decision making was necessary to one focused more on multiple voices, from a situation where no one outside his immediate family could be trusted to one where it is better to draw on talents from all areas of society, from a situation where decisive, and often ruthless, action was necessary, to one where the protections and norms of a society built on laws has become far more important.

It is crucial to note that Masoud Barzani has made these changes better than many others in equivalent situations. He could easily have become a strongman and a dictator, yet he has avoided both, moving gradually towards a more open and democratic society in Kurdistan. Part of the reason for this is that he has seen first hand what such regimes can do, both under the British as a child and then later, tellingly, under the

Ba'athists. He had seen the centralisation of control under Saddam following a successful revolution, and had seen the mass murder that it could lead to. Masoud Barzani has had as much reason as anyone, therefore, to avoid the temptations that come with his role.

In this sense, one of the most important things that he has done in his political career was to step down. It was, in a lot of ways, the moment when he showed most clearly that he was more interested in the wellbeing of Kurdistan than simply in his own power or advancement. When he stepped down as president, he showed that he was willing to put Kurdistan first, stepping away to stop further advances from the Baghdad government and so protect the region's people. Perhaps he had also recognised that there was nothing more he could do to push towards independence, and, recognising that the cause was more important than himself, he moved away from it so that could continue to progress.

What will happen now though, for Masoud Barzani? He is no longer in a formal political role, and there is little evidence that he wishes to begin a career in, for example, business. Will he disappear completely from the political scene in Kurdistan? Will he simply retire? Alternatively, will he seek to have some kind of continuing, informal role in the fortunes of the would be nation?

As difficult as it will be for him after a lifetime involved with Kurdish politics, it seems important that he does step back completely at this point. To be taken seriously as a region making further progress to open, fair, transparent democracy, there cannot be the figure of a former president in the background, appearing to call the shots of the government. Masoud Barzani's continuing role as party head of the KDP makes this somewhat hard to avoid, but where possible, he should seek to distance himself from continued involvement in the control of the country.

The role that he *can* play is a symbolic one, standing above and apart from the details of everyday politics as a reminder of the cause of Kurdish independence. This is potentially an important role, because it can provide a pure focus on the need to push forward towards eventual independence, without the complications that inevitably arise from day to day politics. The president's role is complicated by defence and domestic concerns, by the need to balance a thousand different elements. As someone beyond the realm of politics, Masoud Barzani may be able to more clearly keep the message he presents focused on that singular outcome. It is a role he is uniquely suited for. As we have seen in this biography, from the moment he was born, Masoud Barzani was steeped in the symbolism of independence. It is something he is well placed to carry forward.

Perhaps a more difficult question is where he fits into the list of the major figures within his own family, in a lineage that has included Sheik Mamoud Barzani and Sheik Ahmad, Mullah Mustafa Barzani, and now President Nechirvan Barzani. It is probably an unfair game to ask which of them counts as the greatest in the broad sweep of history, but we can at least seek to understand the different roles that they have played.

Sheik Mamoud Barzanji's role is probably best described as being the first to truly rise up in the modern era in the cause of his tribe and the surrounding area's independence. Sheik

Ahmad went a stage further, with his principles starting to forge inter-tribal connections and a broader front on which to fight back. Mullah Mustafa Barzani was probably the first to lead a rebellion that was about all of Kurdistan, and was in many ways the first to see the importance of aspects such as symbolic power and international influence. President Nechirvan Barzani promises to be the first of a new breed of politically oriented, democratically focused, modern figures who will make it so obvious that Kurdistan is a functioning country that even a sceptical world may agree to its reality.

Masoud Barzani's legacy is more complex. He was utterly bound up with conflict for much of his life, but he was also the first Barzani for whom that conflict was never about an occupying British force, but purely about the imposition of control from Baghdad. He was a war leader who understood the exigencies of such situations, and who was fundamentally shaped by some of the fears and problems that came with being constantly hunted by the government. He has taken on some of the hardest fights that the people of Kurdistan have ever had to face, and has seen horrors that have eclipsed anything that afflicted the Kurds in his father or grandfather's lifetime. Yet he has also been a political leader in a democratic state, seeking to act through the ballot box rather than with the bullet. He has sought and received democratic mandates for his actions, and has been a part of the opening out of Kurdistan's society into something far more tolerant than the countries that surround it.

In this, it might be best to see him as a bridge between the old and the new for Kurdistan. While the idea of a separate region (let alone a country), was met with violence, Kurdistan needed military leaders, guerrillas and strategists who could act decisively with only their charismatic authority to back them. Now that it has become a functioning state in all but name, it needs politicians and organisers who have the courage to give in when the political situation goes against them, knowing that it is for the benefit of the system as a whole, and that things will eventually swing back their way. It is to Masoud Barzani's credit that he has been able to play both roles, and been able to transition, over time, from one to the other.

This should not be underestimated, as it is a transition that leaders in many emerging countries have been unable to manage. Unable to let go of the past, or perhaps seeing rewards for years of service, their times have been marked by scandals and authoritarianism. Masoud Barzani has been gradually been moving away from this, and in doing so has set a course that Kurdistan will hopefully continue to be able to progress along.

Representing Transitions

Let us explore this in between role for Masoud Barzani further. The essence of it is simple: his father was an essentially military figure, while Nechirvan Barzani is a modern political one. Masoud Barzani, though, was the one to bridge that gap. He was one of the first to understand the need for coherent and consistent political structures, even in a phase when many members of what became the KDP were unable to enter Iraq. He played a key role in securing control of those structures along with his brother Idris Barzani. He helped to establish elements such as the Parastin Agency that would later help to secure Kurdistan as a region, and played a vital role in the peshmerga, but also held the presidency of Kurdistan and helped to safeguard the rights of minority groups. He stood up to Baghdad militarily, but when the time came to do something else, he was the one out in the world, advancing Kurdistan's cause through the medium of international relations.

In general, the arc of Masoud Barzani's life has been from a more military start to a more political later phase. This is often true of major figures in emerging democracies. His earlier years were marked by his involvement in the violent attempted revolutions that saw Kurdistan at odds with the Baghdad government again and again, and we cannot doubt his effectiveness in these phases as a commander. He knew when to strike and when to pull back, managed to get the respect of a fighting force that would never have given him that respect simply based on who he was.

Yet even in that period, he played just as much of a role as a political envoy, a negotiator, and a creator of structures that would pass the test of time. He was picked to be a part of the negotiating party in 1970 for the deal that emerged with Baghdad, had an important role to play in negotiating Kurdish involvement after the Iran revolution, was a vital aide to his father in his later years. Even before Kurdistan became the autonomous region that it is today, he was balancing political roles alongside the military decisions that he had to make in fighting a larger and better equipped enemy.

He was crucial in the days after Kurdistan was able to break away from Saddam's control, and even more important in the days after Iraq's dictator finally fell. He was the leader

THE BRINK OF FREEDOM

that Kurdistan needed in that moment, able to both keep it safe militarily, and also play a vital part in the construction of its constitution. A purely political leader wouldn't have been able to survive the military threats that were levelled at Kurdistan in that period. A purely military leader wouldn't have been able to build stable political and social structures that allowed Kurdistan to develop into a safe and consistent place to live in.

Even in recent times, we have been able to see him bridging the gap between the political and the military. During the fight against ISIS, he was an ostensibly political leader, and that was vital to managing the humanitarian crisis, yet he also had a crucial role in managing the actions of the peshmerga to ensure that Kurdistan remained safe.

This balancing act, therefore, has been crucial to Kurdistan. In the future, it is likely that leaders will be more purely political, with greater separation between the military and civil authorities. This is likely to be beneficial in terms of the democratic functioning of Kurdistan, yet in his lifetime, Masoud Barzani was exactly the balance that Kurdistan required.

Symbolism

Symbolism has been another key theme of Masoud Barzani's life. From the very beginning, when he was wrapped in the flag of the Mahabad Republic as a baby, he has been entangled in the symbolism of the cause of independence. Like his father before him, he has, in many ways, come to represent that cause in people's minds, so that it is hard to think of Kurdistan's independence movement without thinking of Masoud Barzani.

In his life, Masoud Barzani has recognised this power, with the result that he has made crucial efforts to ensure Kurdistan's cultural survival alongside its political and military protection. He has understood that it is possible for Kurdistan's opponents to wipe it away simply by reducing its distinctiveness, as easily as by destroying it with weaponry.

In his early life, he was a symbol of hope for the future of the cause, with his presence close to his father suggesting that Kurdistan's independence might well lie in the next generation, even if it could not be brought about immediately. As he grew, he became a symbol of the involvement of his family at the heart of the movement, being first a peshmerga and then involved as a representative for his father in numerous talks around the world.

In the middle of his life, he became the figure around whom the cause of resistance to an oppressive regime coalesced, and in a situation marked by limited information and access to communications technology among the general population, such a symbolic figure was important. It gave a clear person to look to for direction, and for action against the threats that Kurdistan faced.

That symbolism became even more important after the fall of Saddam, with Masoud Barzani helping to hold Kurdistan together through his personality and his presence until it was possible to get more permanent structures in place. In such a void, it would have been easy for Kurdistan to splinter into a hundred pieces, each belonging to some faction or other. In practice, only two main blocs emerged, because of the presence of their leaders, and Masoud Barzani's charisma and presence was important in bringing about some level of unity between them. His commitment to the idea of Kurdistan helped to ensure that it became a reality as a political entry.

As president, he has been a crucial figure both on a political level and a symbolic one. He has been important in giving Kurdistan a sense of direction, keeping the focus towards independence, and the movement of its politics in a consistent direction. His symbolic power there was vital in holding Kurdistan together during the conflict with ISIS, and in its disputes with the Baghdad government.

Yet there was also a sense in which Masoud Barzani was bound by the symbolism around him. Broadly, everyone knew what was likely to happen in the wake of Kurdistan's referendum, and numerous observers had warned about the dangers that might follow. Masoud Barzani, as an intelligent man, must also have known that there was a risk of military action. Yet, having been committed to independence for so much of his life, he couldn't avoid having the referendum on it. It was potentially his last chance to do so, and there was no way that he could *not* live up to the symbol that he had made himself into.

Systems

While we can discuss Masoud Barzani's symbolic value, we must balance that theme with another: the role he played in creating systems that were bigger than any one man. While he has been held up throughout his life as an example of the key figure around whom events have revolved, he has also been responsible on numerous occasions for setting up systems that could function without such a figure.

When he was young, for example, he and his brother Idris Barzani played key roles together in setting up aspects of the KDP's political structures, effectively creating a government in exile in years when Saddam Hussein's government proved too much of a threat for key Barzani figures to be present in Kurdistan. He also played a key role in the development of the Parastin Agency, which assisted in the security of Kurdistan, and later fed into its current internal security arrangements.

Later, his voice was crucial in the development of the structures of modern Kurdistan, first through his role in the 1970 negotiations that established it in principle, then in the talks that produced Kurdistan's constitution. In many ways, his role in those talks represented something much bigger than his role as the president. As Kurdistan's president, and now as the KDP's leader after his presidency, he has had significant impacts within the domain of Kurdistan's politics, yet in his role building systems and shaping the constitution, he helped to define the limits and shape of those politics.

It is a role that is vital, and that will have impacts on Kurdistan's politics for generations to come, even after the last of the policies that he enacted in his lifetime has passed. He has influenced the path of this generation through his direct work as president, but the structures he helped found in Kurdistan will influence its course for many more.

This aspect is also reflected in terms of balancing the symbolic value he has held. Symbolic value is intrinsically linked to an individual, but in helping to create systems within Kurdistan, Masoud Barzani also helped to create politics within it that have the potential to be bigger than any one person.

That is one of the biggest elements of his presidency, as noted in the section on tradition. Masoud Barzani has formed a bridge between the more traditional and the more modern, starting off as a figure holding things together through his personality in the mould of his father, but moving towards a more systems based approach that holds the potential for the efficient transfer of power within Kurdistan, and for the gradual development of increasing democracy and rights there.

In one sense, stepping down as Kurdistan's president has been the biggest step of all in that regard. In doing so, and in allowing Nechirvan Barzani to take over as president, he has made the point that Kurdistan's politics are bigger than just one man, even him. It is a sign of the extent to which he has always put Kurdistan first, beyond his own well being, and certainly beyond what would be easiest.

Responsibility

Another key theme of Masoud Barzani's life has been that of responsibility. Almost from the moment he was born, the weight of responsibility has rested on his shoulders. There has been responsibility to live up to his family name, responsibility for key roles at a young age, responsibility for the rest of his party, and as president, responsibility for an entire region.

The first layer of that responsibility came as Masoud Barzani was a child. There was an inherent responsibility that came from factors beyond his control, from his family name, from his father, and from the symbolic value that those around his family attached to him. From a very early age, he would have been aware that he was meant to be a part of something bigger than himself. We have speculated on whether he was able to have even a brief semblance of a normal childhood, but in truth, that was impossible long term. He didn't have the experiences that most children would have had, or had them in a different way, knowing that there were more important things he was already linked with.

From a very early age, he knew what his life was going to be. Certainly, from the moment his father returned in 1958, it was clear that he would never have a life like anyone else again. More responsibility quickly followed, first with those of a peshmerga, and then as one of his father's key aides and emissaries.

Even from his teen years, Masoud Barzani has been faced with decisions that have meant life or death for those around him. Commanding other peshmerga, his every decision had the potential to result in their deaths if he got them wrong. When he was negotiating on Kurdistan's behalf at the behest of his father, his decisions could, and did, shape the direction of Kurdistan for generations to come.

Yet the phases when Masoud Barzani has had responsibility have in some ways been the easier ones for him, since the ones when things have been out of his control have been amongst the darkest and most dangerous times for Kurdistan. During the Anfal, Masoud Barzani's fighters were engaged against Saddam's troops, but it was a time when he had little or no control over what happened. It was also a time that reinforced the importance of what he and his party were doing, showing that working towards independence was about Kurdish survival rather than just any matter of political organisation.

As president of an emerging democracy, responsibility has rested on Masoud Barzani in a way that it might not have elsewhere, because there has been a tendency in such places to focus on the personality of the leader, and to see the things being done in a nation as being about them personally. For Masoud Barzani, this added to the pressure on him, with the awareness that he had to be on top of every emerging situation, because it would all be seen as his responsibility.

In some ways, the ultimate expression of this responsibility came with the referendum. Even though it was something that the whole of Kurdistan had been working towards for years, and even though it was something where virtually the whole of Kurdistan was involved, and in favour of independence, it was viewed as very much Masoud Barzani's personal project. He was the driving force behind much of it, but it was treated as if no one else was involved in the process.

Yet, in its wake, he *took* responsibility. He was the one who stood down as part of the process that followed it, and he was the one who sought to ensure that the aftermath did not harm Kurdistan too greatly.

Yet even as his presidency has come to an end, the responsibilities have not for Masoud Barzani. His role as the leader of the KDP has continued, while others have called for his intervention on an informal basis in other areas of Iraq. In part, this is simply how politics work in the region, where no one truly retires, but it is also an extension of his sense of responsibility towards the world around him, a responsibility that has driven him to so much through his career.

Uprisings

One key element of Masoud Barzani's life has been the uprisings he has been involved in. Like his father before him, he has been involved in many conflicts against the Baghdad government over the years, usually with the same causes, and unfortunately, usually with the same shape. These conflicts have formed a key pattern in his life, but also suggest a pattern in Kurdistan's relations with Baghdad that may need to be changed by future leaders, if it is even possible to do so.

The conflicts have all come about in broadly the same way, being over Kurdistan's desire for independence, set against Baghdad's desire to hold onto it, and in particular the oil resources within it. Kurdistan, meanwhile, has been aware of the need for those resources to pay for the infrastructure and other expenditure needed of a state. It is a direct opposition of interests that is hard to work out or find a compromise for, with the result that essentially the same conflict has happened repeatedly in Masoud Barzani's life.

Typically, the situation begins with a background level of grievances from one or both sides. The desire of Kurdistan to be independent is hardly disguised, while Baghdad has exerted constant pressure to try to make Kurdistan more closely controlled. That, though, has rarely been the spark for conflict, only the fuel for it once it begins.

The move to an actual confrontation has typically come in the context of other conflicts. In his father and grandfather's lives, these were the aftermaths of the two world wars, but later, other periods of instability would also play a role, including coups within Iraq and Iran, conflicts between those powers, the international fight against Saddam, and most recently, the conflict with ISIS. Typically, the Kurdish forces have rec-ognised an opportunity in such events to either gain allies for the fight ahead, or to face only a part of Baghdad's military forces as the rest are distracted by another conflict. In the case of the referendum, for example, it is clear that Masoud Barzani made the calculated gamble that Baghdad was too weakened by its conflict with ISIS to dispute independence if it happened, that the eyes of the world were too clearly focused on Iraq for Baghdad to strike, and that there was too much chaos already for its international partners to want Baghdad to cause more.

In the event though, this did not prove to be the case, because of the third typical phase: an abandonment by Kurdistan's international allies. The international allies Kurdistan has thought would support it in its attempts at independence have typically not been involved in its affairs to bring that about. Instead, they have been seeking to use Kurdistan as a proxy in the region to achieve their aims, and the word 'proxy' is important here. It implies an initial unwillingness on their part to do their own fighting in the region, which then makes it exceptionally unlikely that they will wish to do Kurdistan's for it. It means that when violence comes, they do not interfere. In the case of the referendum, America and various European countries made it clear that while they were happy Kurdistan was fighting ISIS on their behalf, they were not going to inter-vene when Baghdad sent tanks north.

The fourth phase has been that retaliation in force by Baghdad, coming again and again throughout Kurdistan's recent history, and always dangerous because Baghdad, even today, holds an advantage in terms of things like heavy armour and air support.

The fifth component has always been the reaction of the countries around Kurdistan, either intervening directly, or closing their borders, or putting in place trade embargoes.

This combination of factors has been consistent in the conflicts in Masoud Barzani's life, and it is important that we identify them, just as we identify why he felt that it was important to strive for independence anyway. That can be explained by a number of things: the feeling that a particular situation may have represented a better opportunity than those before, the feeling that Kurdistan was more prepared than before, and of course, the enduring importance of the cause to which Masoud Barzani has dedicated his life: independence.

To achieve that cause, those who come after Masoud Barzani will have to learn lessons from his life, understanding the factors preventing Kurdistan from achieving such independence before. Only with such an understanding will it be possible to break the cycle of revolts being crushed by overwhelming force, and to finally enact the will of Kurdistan's people on the subject.

Could Anyone Else Have Done This

We asked a similar question in relation to his brother, Idris Barzani, but it is useful to ask it here too: could anyone else have done all that Masoud Barzani has done in his career?

Certainly, there are people who could have done some of it. There have been good military commanders in the past, and those who have led the peshmerga to victories in individual conflicts. There have been leaders who have worked towards independence for their countries, and some have even succeeded. There have been leaders who have made the transition from military figures to civilian leaders, and who have helped to produce democratic norms in their countries. There have been those who have stood for particular causes, and been the symbolic centres of wider movements.

Yet the numbers of those who have done more than one of these things are far smaller, and only a few figures in history have done all of them. Faced with that, *could* anyone else have filled the roles involved?

We could say that some of it is simply the position that Masoud Barzani found himself in. It might be possible to argue that he achieved all of these things *because* he was the son of Mustafa Barzani, and because he became the leader of the KDP. Those things meant that he was at the heart of a conflict that required a mixture of the military and the political, while the circumstances arising from the Anfal and the two gulf wars pushed Kurdistan more in the direction of autonomy. In theory, any leader might have been carried along with that to an extent, yet we know from examples elsewhere in the world that struggles for independence, and genocides, can produce very different outcomes in different places.

We could also say that part of the reason that Masoud Barzani has achieved all of the things he has is because he has been prepared his whole life to do exactly that. From the moment he was born, he was prepared to be a leader. He was provided with opportunities to lead, and to fulfil key roles. Yet we can suggest that was as much of a burden as a privilege. All his life, Masoud Barzani has had to live up to the expectations placed on him. For every supposed advantage, there has been a threat to match it, for every position of authority, decisions that meant life or death for those around him.

Of course, we could turn this around and ask a different question: could Masoud Barzani have done anything else? In some ways, it seems obvious that his skills as a leader and as a fighter might have allowed him to become engaged in a cause anywhere in the world, while there is no reason to think that he could not have been a success in some other walk of life. Yet the things that brought him to that point, the training and the circumstances that gave him experience, also pushed him in the direction of Kurdistan's cause. The very things that made him who he was also put him in a position where he couldn't be anyone else. His commitment to Kurdistan's cause has always been a fundamental part of who he is.

So yes, there are elements of Masoud Barzani's story that have stemmed from the situation around him, or from the ways in which he was pushed into circumstances through the expectations of others, yet we cannot say that things would have turned out identically for someone else. Masoud Barzani has achieved all that he has in his life partly through circumstance, and partly through the efforts of those around him, but we cannot deny that much of it was about him. It would not have turned out the same way for anyone else, and Kurdistan would have been the poorer for it.

The Future

What does the future hold for Masoud Barzani after the past has contained so much? To understand that, we need to understand something about the nature of politics in the Middle East in general, about the nature of retirement, and about the ongoing situation in and around Kurdistan.

Masoud Barzani has officially stepped down as president of Kurdistan, so that at the time of writing Nechirvan Barzani holds the post. It means that he will no longer have the level of official control that he once had, and that he will not be able to set the agenda for Kurdistan in quite the same way anymore. He will not be able to help decide what the laws will be in Kurdistan, or to make official decisions on behalf of the autonomous region.

Yet it would be a mistake to think that his political career is finished. He will still continue as the leader of the KDP, having a considerable amount of influence over events within the region. He will continue to be the face of the region, and will continue to talk to officials from around the world. It should be remembered that, while that might look strange to outsiders, it is normal practice in the Middle East. The practice elsewhere of leaders stepping down completely and retiring from public life is less common, and it is usual for there to be an overall party leader, with other leaders coming around that.

It is hard to imagine Masoud Barzani embracing the kind of retirement seen in much of the rest of the world. Indeed, it is hard to see why he should have to, while around the world, former leaders are starting think tanks, charitable foundations, and trying to influence politics from the background. The era of the quiet retirement, if it ever truly existed, is long gone.

It seems undeniable that Masoud Barzani will continue to influence KDP policy to some extent, with a continued push towards independence in the long run. This is valuable, because it means that the policies involved will be informed by the values built during his life, and by the events the people of Kurdistan have experienced during his lifetime.

The value of that experience can be seen in the calls for him to help elsewhere. During the violence in the south of Iraq, there were calls for him to help by stepping in as a leader able to hold together disparate parts of a fractured whole. It was a moment that showed just how vital he had become, not just to Kurdistan, but to the whole region around it.

He will continue to be important, both because the structures he helped to create now shape the ways in which Kurdistan does business, and because symbolically, he has *become* Kurdistan, or at least the cause of Kurdistan's independence. It is impossible to think about that cause without thinking about him, just as it became impossible to do so with his father. This will only be increased by whatever efforts he continues to make in that direction.

More importantly though, Masoud Barzani has helped to set the direction of Kurdistan's politics and society. He has served as a bridge between older ways and newer, more progressive approaches. By doing so, he has ensured that it will continue to head down that path, and down the route towards independence. His last attempt at it, with the referendum, may not have succeeded, but years from now, people will look back, see the situation Kurdistan has reached, and understand clearly that there is no way it could have gotten there without Masoud Barzani. He has served as a symbol for Kurdistan, has shaped it, and will continue to do so for years to come.

ABOUT THE AUTHOR

Davan Yahya Khalil is an author and journalist, originally from Kurdistan and now based in the UK. Having completed a Masters degree in law, he runs the publication the New Mail.

In books such as Kurdistan: Genocide and Rebirth, Kurdistan: The Road to Independence and The Idea of Kurdistan, he has become a key voice exploring issues and figures relating to the region, setting them in their historical and political context while exploring the possibilities for their future.